DEMOCRACY AND THE INTERSECTION
OF RELIGION AND TRADITIONS

Democracy and the Intersection of Religion and Traditions

The Reading of John Dewey's Understanding of Democracy and Education

ROSA BRUNO-JOFRÉ, JAMES SCOTT
JOHNSTON, GONZALO JOVER, AND
DANIEL TRÖHLER

McGill-Queen's University Press
Montreal & Kingston • London • Ithaca

© McGill-Queen's University Press 2010
ISBN 978-0-7735-3784-2 (cloth)
ISBN 978-0-7735-3785-9 (paper)

Legal deposit fourth quarter 2010
Bibliothèque nationale du Québec

Printed in Canada on acid-free paper that is 100% ancient forest free
(100% post-consumer recycled), processed chlorine free.

McGill-Queen's University Press acknowledges the support of the Canada
Council for the Arts for our publishing program. We also acknowledge the
financial support of the Government of Canada through the Canada Book
Fund for our publishing activities.

Library and Archives Canada Cataloguing in Publication

Democracy and the intersection of religion and traditions : the reading of
John Dewey's understanding of democracy and education / Rosa Bruno-
Jofre ... [et al.].

Includes bibliographical references and index.
ISBN 978-0-7735-3784-2 (bound) – ISBN 978-0-7735-3785-9 (pbk)

1. Dewey, John, 1859–1952 – Influence. 2. Democracy and education
– China. 3. Democracy and education – Spain. 4. Democracy and education – Latin America. I. Bruno-Jofré, Rosa del Carmen, 1946–

LB875.D5D46 2011   370.11'5   C2010-903873-8

This book was typeset by True to Type in 10/14 Sabon

Contents

DEMOCRACY AND THE INTERSECTION OF RELIGION AND TRADITIONS

Introduction

ROSA BRUNO-JOFRÉ, JAMES SCOTT JOHNSTON,
GONZALO JOVER, AND DANIEL TRÖHLER

John Dewey's educational thought began to receive world-wide attention immediately after publication of *School and Society* in 1899. Scholars are only now beginning to chronicle and interpret this phenomenon. Recent books and articles attest to the significance of this new scholarship.[1] In this recent work, a central question asked of Dewey and Dewey's uptake in differing political, social, cultural, linguistic, and bureaucratic contexts is, whither democracy?[2] This book begins with an analysis of Dewey's background and his affinity with Protestant ideas as a way of opening avenues to understand why Dewey, in spite of what most philosophers refer to as his "naturalistic metaphysics," seems to leave room for religion and religious experience. The three case studies in this book analyse how Dewey's educational ideas and democratic ideals have been configured and how they were taken up and interpreted in different specific historical spaces. The intersection of religion as a lens or as a context emerged variously in all of the studies.

The approach we take in our discussions of Dewey's uptake is to understand it as a matter of configurations. Configurations as we construe them are spaces that historical phenomena take when inquired into. These spaces open up to other spaces in further uptakes. They are heuristic rather than explanatory. We use them in order to distinguish, relate, and, ultimately, understand various historical phenomena. Configuration allows us to articulate spaces within which there are multiple connections between discourses and political connections, many of which are contradictory but form other configurations within a larger heuristic. New configurations arise out of older ones; within a configuration, new configurations form. The configurations we talk about involve the notion of exportation and the articulation of religion and democracy, and are the result of the intersection of multiple historical forces specific to the spaces we study.

Our studies made it clear that in the process of building a notion of a new polity and a new education, Dewey's readers were not concerned with maintaining consistency with Dewey's broader philosophy, particularly with his notion of democracy as a "mode of associated living, of conjoint, communicated experience" in which people work together to solve each other's problems, using the tools of (social) inquiry.[3]

Daniel Tröhler's chapter, "'Socialism or Protestant Democracy?' The Pragmatist Response to the Perils of Metropolis and Modern Industry in the Late Nineteenth Century," begins the book. The concept of configuration, for Tröhler, makes evident that pragmatism itself is an idiosyncratic perception of the world, a specific mode of thinking resulting from the tensions between specific ideals of life and social and economic conditions of life. It allows him to reconstruct the generation of pragmatist thinking as an intellectual configuration that resulted from the tension between specific Protestant interpretations of actual living conditions in the cities and the social vision of American Protestantism, the "City upon a Hill." Pragmatism becomes a genuine option to other interpretations of these conditions and therefore to the different solutions, such as socialism, that they propose to deal with the perceived crisis at the *fin de siècle*. Tröhler argues that pragmatism is in accordance with older Protestant concepts in which perceived social problems were "educationalized." In other words, pragmatism is essentially an educational approach, deriving from the assumption that education can solve fundamental problems. Although Dewey's thinking is not religious in the ecclesiastic sense, it is still an expression of the secular Protestantism dominating the American mentality.

The following three chapters examine how and why Dewey's thought was interpreted in various ways and even "mutilated" according to the intellectual and ideological configurations that served as mediating formations. The notion of configuration helps us examine how and why readings of Dewey and the uptake of his ideas took such an eclectic character. The metaphor of "traveling libraries" and the phrase "indigenous foreigner," both well known in educational circles, have inspired the recent work of educational historians examining modernity and how Dewey's ideas have travelled. However, we concluded that the notion of configuration would open ways to heuristically delve into the nuances, impurities, articulations, and/or juxtapositions of Dewey's ideas with beliefs, habits, and ideas characterizing the discursive spaces.

James Scott Johnston's chapter, "Must Democratic Aims and Means Ally? A Historical-Philosophical Answer from an Unlikely Context," discusses Dewey in the context of his lengthy visit to China. What is unique about Dewey's experience in China (aside from the evident enjoyment he remarks on in numerous writings) is his sustained engagement with the American public about Chinese public sentiment through venues such as the magazines *The Dial* and the *New Republic*. This writing provides us with a unique opportunity – to see how American understanding of Chinese affairs as interpreted through Dewey meshed with Chinese understandings of Dewey. As Johnston discusses, there is a disconnect between what Dewey reports back to the United States, and the situation in China. This discrepancy occurs because Dewey, who neither spoke nor read Chinese, was unable to witness at first-hand the political and social climate of China. He was at the mercy of his translators and interpreters, who were themselves politically positioned. An interesting feature emerged – readings of Dewey as *hostile* to Chinese traditions, including Confucianism and Buddhism – which is *not* grounded in Dewey's writing. This leads, paradoxically, to Dewey's message regarding the importance of democratic means aligning with democratic ends and taking a back seat to the rhetoric of social and political overhaul.

Gonzalo Jover's chapter, "The Readings of John Dewey in Spain in the Early Twentieth Century: Reconciling Pragmatism and Transcendence," examines how Dewey was read by the Spanish Institución Libre de Ensenanza (Free Teaching Institute) within the context of the Catholic debate that took place in Spain during the first decades of the twentieth century and beyond. During this period, discussion of epistemological problems was abandoned and social and political issues became prominent. Jover concludes that the Dewey that interested Spanish thinkers was not Dewey the philosopher, but the Dewey who could provide useful ideas to modernize education, the Dewey of functional psychology and learning by doing, meaning that Dewey's educational ideas were stripped of their philosophical bases. Previous configurations made possible the interpretation and adoption of new ideas, but they also set mediating parameters to the way in which those new ideas were read.

Rosa Bruno-Jofré's chapter, "To Those in 'Heathen Darkness': Deweyan Democracy and Education in the American Interdenominational Configuration – The Case of the Committee on Cooperation in Latin America," examines the creation of this Committee (with offices in New York!) and its discourses, as narrated in the reports of the two major Congresses organized by the Committee: the Panama Congress of 1916 and the Montevideo Congress of 1925. The contextual frame of reference is provided by the ideology of Pan-Americanism embraced by the leaders of the Committee (ideology opposed by intellectuals and left-wing leaders in Latin America), the strong influence of radical social gospellers, and the overall intersection of religious education that integrated pragmatists' ideas and Dewey's ideas with the social gospel. The discourses were part of a synthetic yet unstable configuration of democracy and education understood in relation to spiritual redemption at both the individual and social level. The Committee's aims were part of a prophetic project to reconstruct the Latin American polity in which democracy and Dewey's notion of democracy became synonymous with Protestant liberal Christianity. The missionaries' work and discourses were framed by the presence in Latin America of political projects and social movements that became nationalistic and/or politically radical.

Various differences and distinctions in reading Dewey are notable when one contrasts the four chapters. For example, the translators/interpreters in China took the shape of a vanguard who read Dewey through the lenses of their political project. Dewey's writing back to the United States during his extended visit to China forged a unique connection between the China Dewey saw and reported on and the China Dewey's interpreters and translators led him to see. In Spain, the Institución Libre de Ensenanza formed a political intellectual vanguard that read Dewey at various times and in the process severed his educational theories from pragmatism or even articulated Dewey's educational ideas with a notion of transcendence. The missionaries working in Latin America also acted as a political vanguard, carriers of a redemptive liberal, democratic project. The Committee on Cooperation was expected to build cooperation among denominations and ties of solidarity within the American continent, with the United States as point of reference. The chapters raise serious questions about the consistency of readings of Dewey in terms of his account of democracy and the interpretations of his philosophy that informed their educational theories.

Within this context, a major issue emerged in the research: the exportation of a notion of democracy and the role of the public – major political themes of our time. We use the public in Dewey's sense as an expression for the mass of peoples intelligently inquiring into matters of community and national interest. The problematic includes the alignment of ends and means so relevant to Dewey. Our studies demonstrate that the understanding of democratic means becomes embedded in the cultural dynamics of relations in specific situations. The adoption of Dewey's notions of democracy and education progress through various processes of both transformation and re-articulation in various configurations. In the case of China, Dewey's writings to his American public bore little resemblance to what Chinese learned publics were hearing and reading. The self-transformative nature of democratic education is a specific subtheme that is explored in relation to China. In the case of the Free Teaching Institute and his main Spanish translators/interpreters, Barnes and Luzuriaga, Dewey's educational notions were separated from their pragmatist grounding and incorporated into a recreated and kaleidoscopic configuration. In the case of the Committee on Cooperation in Latin America and its missionary concern, there are interesting justapositions generated by the influence of George. A. Coe, translator of Dewey's ideas in light of the Social Gospel, the exportation of a notion of democracy embedded in a discourse of redemption and American values, and the attempt by some leaders of the Committee to rely on the ideology of Pan-Americanism (contested by more radical social gospellers). Our studies point toward the historical limits to the exportation of democracy.

Our most intriguing working theme is the intersection of religion in the uptake of Dewey and its bearing on the understanding of democratic education. In the case of China, Dewey is further fragmented by his interlocutors and translators. While certainly no partisan of theocracy, Dewey was interpreted as hostile to Chinese traditions, including Confucianism and Buddhism. This in fact was not the case, as we see from Dewey's articles for American consumption. The presence of Catholicism in the Spanish belief system along with idealism led the leaders of the Free Teaching Institute to a notion of a neutral school that compensated for the lack of confessional foundations with a transcendental vision of the humane. Religion was evident in the discourse of the missionary Congresses embracing the social gospel and the scholarship of George Coe, a religious educator and Dewey scholar, who developed the concept of "democracy of God." The case studies illustrate ways of amalgamating Dewey's notion of democracy with specific configurations emerging from each context. Hybrid configurations, though not necessarily logically sustainable ones, emerged. In some cases, these were neither politically nor intellectually sustainable. They were transient, temporary, or simply practical.

Dewey's lectures and writings were taken up by his translators in a manner and tone that was foreign to Dewey. The irony here is that Dewey concentrated on the *means* by which democracies formed: through conjoint, communicative experiences. Only by problem-finding and sharing in communicative networks could democratic ends be secured. What makes a practice anti-democratic is the inability of the public (the stakeholders) to share in the decision-making processes leading up to the implementation of the practice. This can occur in many ways. In the case of the Spanish context, there was a concern about the place of the public in political life, as shown in Ortega y Gasset's famous discussion on *The Revolt of the Masses*. Democracy was linked to the modernization of education. Dewey was read in support of this goal, but in the reading democracy remains an external aim. In the case of China, there was yet no clearly identifiable public, beyond the vanguard scholars and student-led movements, to ask. While it was certainly the case that the student-led movement, university officials, and other, 'progressive' elements wanted democratic change, there was not yet a nascent public to whom this change was directed. In the case of missionary congresses attempting to generate cooperation in the plan to develop a new polity in Latin America, the majority of the missionaries attending were American, not Latin American nationals, and the dominant language was English. Meanwhile, the schools were, by and large, their laboratories. The missionaries used Dewey's rhetoric of the 'public,' but they had difficulties in filtering this down to them even as they realized that the missions had to acquire a national identity. They were also aware of the institutional political limits in Latin American countries. Furthermore, the notion of the public was coloured by urban, middle-class American Protestantism, while there was a disconnect from the lived experiences of the publics the congresses had in mind. In any situation in which the public is not given a say, including a say in the decision(s) leading up to implementation, the practice is anti-democratic in light of Dewey's philosophy, regardless of whether a democratic 'end' is envisioned. *There are, properly speaking, no democratic ends that follow from non-democratic means.*

Creating the conditions for democratic means is very difficult. It demands participatory democracy in its fullest approximation and it may require attention to the foreseeable drawbacks attending a direct, democratic, governing model.[4] Dewey foresaw what was needed; he turned to the schools for the creation of a "democracy in miniature," and hoped that in the future children would grow to become the sorts of social beings that would form a "great community," with confidence in procedural and representative government to secure and safeguard freedoms, not obfuscate them.[5] Dewey was perhaps naïve in thinking that the great bureaucracies could be dismantled and the power of public decision-making returned to the people. Walter Lippmann, Dewey's famous arch-rival, certainly thought so.[6] However, Dewey is correct in the need for the dismantling of such bureaucracies (or oligarchies, or even vanguard approaches) *if* the sort of public he envisions is to prosper.

It becomes evident in the studies that the cultural context in part drives the specific democratic practices that then follow. As differing contexts will require differing practices in order to produce a democratic mode of associated living, a democratic mode of associated living must consider context. The sorts of practices that emerged have to do with patterns of communication, the system of schools, political regimes, and the presence of Catholic (vs Protestant/secular) influence, language, and the necessary understandings of how to work across cultural differences. We should not expect that a democratic education in one nation would be isomorphic with a democratic education in another, although we should expect that a democratic education would adjust itself in whatever context it was placed. Conclusions in this regard would require a great deal of empirical research in actual practices that is beyond the scope of this book.

WHY DEWEY, WHY THEN?

We tried to answer the question of why Dewey's ideas travelled the way they did. This cannot be answered without a satisfactory account of the various understandings of Dewey's interpreters, as well as Dewey's works themselves. As we mentioned earlier, our working method is hermeneutical and contextual and based on the idea of configurations. Often enough, some interpretive configurations do not 'mesh' with other self-understood forms and spaces of those interpreting Dewey. Often, Dewey's ideas are permanently configured or alternatively configured. When this happens, a configuration unbeknownst to those who interpret Dewey arises, paradoxically, and it becomes difficult if not impossible to realize that we are using and appealing to a configuration not of our choosing. Others often note that these forms and spaces are not in keeping with the avowed goals and interests (not to say rhetoric) of the interpretations and use of Dewey's ideas. This happens for a variety of reasons, but two among the most hypothesized are ideology and regimes of discourse.[7]

We can point to various configurations from which and in which philosophical, religious, and political understandings take place. Configurations not only provide us with the capacity to juxtapose alternative conceptions of Dewey's uptake but give us insights into the contexts in which these uptakes themselves took place. As configurations are the shapes, forms, and spaces in which these uptakes and the subsequent historical and philosophical understandings of these uptakes manifest, configurations operate as form or structure, helping to determine what the understanding of Dewey's thoughts and ideas will be, the spaces in which Dewey's thoughts and ideas are developed and contextualized, and the form of the subsequent critical understanding that is partly a product of this taking up, and partly a critical investigation of it.

This brings us back to the benefit of configuration as a heuristic tool. Configuration is helpful because it offers us another means to understand historical phenomena, and does so in a way that accounts for interpretive differences across multiple interlocutors and varying contexts. These include the transnational contexts we are interested in here. Configuration accomplishes this through the following characteristics. First, configurations are bounded or enclosed spaces, which provide shape and form only through these boundaries. We are able to discriminate what properly belongs 'in' the configuration and what belongs 'outside' the configuration, as a result. Without these boundaries, we are unable to discriminate between 'in' and 'out,' and unable to differentiate relevant from irrelevant historical phenomena. Second, configurations provide us with a way to talk fruitfully of changes in time and context. Configurations change. The boundaries are semi-permeable, at least when considered over time. Not unlike Dewey's notion of reconstruction, configurations are vibrant, context-sensitive, and amenable to transformation as new ideas and understandings are developed. What makes these changes possible is the presence of an identifiable configuration. Finally, configurations can be 'nested.' That is to say, configurations are those sorts of heuristic devices that can remain intact even as new configurations, or reconstructed versions of older ones, are produced. For example, we could have a consistent configuration of Dewey's model of democracy and, from this, a further configuration (through interpretation of Dewey's thought) of Dewey's model of democracy. The same, of course, applies to Dewey's own thoughts.

The themes we have introduced, the uptake of Dewey's notion of democracy and education and the intersection of religion, led us to considerations of the consistency of democratic means and ends, the question of religious transcendence and its relationship with democratic theory and practice, and the transformative nature of democracy. These considerations are not arbitrary; rather, they emerged from the sources we consulted and place in relief the shifting natures of configurations. As each of the contexts in which Dewey's thought is interpreted produces different configurations of Dewey, these themes place those accounts in relief. These themes are helpful, then, to see the profound differences but also the similarities with Dewey's thought and with one another. More trenchantly for the matter of interpretation, they help us to see where license is established to deviate from Dewey's thoughts and writings. In certain cases, as we discuss in the chapters, this deviation has self-contradictory implications for Dewey's uptake.

What makes the configurations we rely on for theoretical underpinning unique is the characteristic of *transformation*. Configurations (and the developers of specific configurations) become amenable to correction when we see the connections between earlier configurations and later ones. This is the hermeneutic import of successive interpretations: each configuration owes something to previous configurations, even if in opposition to them. Each configuration is partly a product of past configurations. What it means to say a configuration is transformative is to say that configurations themselves are dynamic products that work to perpetuate new configurations. Note that we are not saying that one configuration contains all that is necessary for another. What makes a configuration transformative is its continual re-construction in new contexts, for new aims and purposes: in short, its re-location in new spaces. A new configuration emerges from the rejection or reconstitution of the old in this new space. Yet this new configuration does not abandon entirely the older configurations in becoming; rather, these older configurations not only form the 'content' of the new, they help to stabilize the new, often through their functioning as points of departure that are re-referenced in giving reasons for the worth of the new configuration. Each configuration is bounded by other configurations that work to construct these configurations further. The possibility of justifying new configurations rests not only with the boundaries of the new space, but with the past configurations out of which it forms. Interpretive justification is thus a loosely circular enterprise.

Each of the three case studies presents configurations developed in the uptake of Dewey's thought, the thought of his interpreters, and our own theoretical lenses. These configurations form the possibility for a truly transnational approach to Dewey's uptake that complements, rather than replaces, travelling and empirical accounts of Dewey's influence. The aim of developing a transnational understanding of Dewey's significance and influence is a bold and important one; it hinges, however, on the ability to delve deeply into the various levels of uptake and the resultant configurations that formed, together with the empirical details of Dewey's influence. With this lacuna filled, the understanding of Dewey's significance for various national and international concerns is placed in further relief and questions of why and how Dewey's thought emerged the way it did in these various contexts are better answered.

NOTES

1 Recent works are Sabhiba Bilgi and Seckin Özsoy, "John Dewey's Travelings into the Project of Turkish Modernity" in *Inventing the Modern Self and John Dewey: Modernities and the Traveling of Pragmatism in Education*, Thomas Popkewitz, ed. (New York: Palgrave MacMillan, 2006); Jürgen Oelkers/Heinz Rhyn, guest eds., "Dewey and European Education – General Problems and Case Studies," in *Studies in Philosophy and Education* 19, nos. 1–2 (2000); and Thomas Popkewitz, "Introduction," in *Inventing the Modern Self and John Dewey: Modernities and the Traveling of Pragmatism in Education*, Thomas Popkewitz, ed. (New York: Palgrave MacMillan, 2006). In the Asian context, see in particular, Sor-hoon Tan and John Whalen-Bridge, eds., *Democracy as Culture* (Albany: SUNY Press, 2008); Sor-hoon Tan, *Confucian Democracy: A Deweyan reconstruction* (Albany: SUNY Press, 2004); Sor-hoon Tan, ed. *Challenging Citizenship* (Aldergate, UK: Ashgate, 2005); Ching-Sze (Jessica) Wang, *John Dewey in China: to Teach and to Learn* (New York: Columbia University Press 2007). See, in addition, many specific books and articles on Dewey's educational thought as well as John Dewey, "Experience and Nature," in *John Dewey: The Later Works, 1925–1952*. Vol. 1, 1925, J. Boydston, ed. (Carbondale: Southern Illinois University Press, 1981).

2 Thomas Popkewitz ed., *Inventing the Modern Self and John Dewey*; Tan and Whalen-Bridge, *Democracy as Culture*. Daniel Tröhler, "The 'Kingdom of God on Earth' and Early Chicago Pragmatism," Educational Theory 56 (2006).

3 John Dewey, "Democracy and Education" in *John Dewey: The Middle Works, 1899–1924*, Vol. 9, 1916, J. Boydston, ed. (Carbondale: Southern Illinois University Press, 1980), p. 91.

4 Other than Dewey, this challenge is best captured by Rousseau:

A democratic government, furthermore, presupposes a number of things that are difficult to unite. First, a very small state in which the people can easily be assembled and each citizen can easily know all the others. Second, a great simplicity of customs and morals, to prevent public affairs from becoming to numerous, and thorny discussions from arising. Third, a high degree of equality in rank and wealth, without which equality in rights and authority could not last long. And finally, little or no luxury, for luxury is either the effect of wealth or makes wealth necessary; it corrupts both the rich and the poor: the former by possessiveness, the latter by covetousness; it sells the country to indolence and vanity; it deprives the state of all its citizens by enslaving some to others, and all to public opinion.

Jean-Jacques Rousseau, "The Social Contract," in *The Social Contract and Later Political Writings* [1762](Cambridge: Cambridge University Press, 1997), 74.

5 John Dewey, *The Public and Its Problems* in *John Dewey: The Later Works, 1925–1952*. Vol. 2, 1925–1927, J. Boydston, ed. (Carbondale: Southern Illinois University Press, 1982).

6 Walter Lippmann, *The Phantom Public* (New Brunswick, NJ: Transactions Publishers, 1993).

7 By ideology, we mean the unconscious or sub-conscious acceptance and projection of a dominant thought-system (often political-economic) into one's interpretative frame. We can talk of framing existing forms and spaces through constructs such as 'discursive regimes' – for example, regimes of truth, or knowledge, or science, or (even) democracy. These regimes are structurally dominant on the discourse in the particular community of language-users involved in the discipline or practice. We can talk, therefore, of subconscious uses of this discourse, internalization of this discourse, and the difficulty new discursive regimes (and alternative languages) have in light of these. Interpretation (as with Critical-Theoretic readings) is always already invested in a discourse that is oppressive from the standpoint of other discourses.

I

Socialism or Protestant Democracy?
The Pragmatist Response to the Perils of Metropolis and Modern Industry in the Late Nineteenth Century[1]

DANIEL TRÖHLER

Pragmatism, a specific mode of thinking, has a number of characteristic elements. One of the core elements is the idea that intelligent behavior is "adaptation of the organism to its surroundings" in order to maintain life.[2] In addition to mere "accommodation," by which the individual assimilates and reproduces the existing environment, adaptation also includes "making over of the environment to meet the new demands on the part of the living individual."[3] While we find accommodation in nature and in primitive societies, progressive societies tend to direct their activities "toward securing an adaptation of the environment to the individual's needs and ends, rather than vice versa ... The individual does not accommodate himself to his environment, but takes the initiative in modifying it to make it over into accord with his own desires and purposes. Only when the environment develops by the active initiative and planning of individuals is progress secured," and we may talk of social progress.[4]

We may use this idea of intelligent adaptation in order to understand why and how pragmatism as a specific mode of thinking emerged. To paraphrase Dewey, pragmatism is an intellectual response, within the context of specific challenges posed by life conditions, that tries to bring these conditions into accord with desires and purposes. This leads to two questions. First, what are the conditions to be met? And second, what are the "desires and purposes"? The conjunction of ideologies (or *Weltanschauungen)*, with their idiosyncratic visions of justice and progress, on one hand and the tangible visibility of life (conditions) on the other is of course a common historical configuration, but when the ideological expectations, hopes, and ambitions differ too much from the conditions (or better, the perception of the conditions) of life, the quest for understanding and change becomes vital. At the end of the nineteenth century European and American cities and the market economy, with its social consequences, had become configurational catalysts in the generation of intellectual and political doctrines. Otto von Bismarck, the first chancellor of the Second German Empire (1871–1918), used a carrot and stick policy to attempt to dissuade German workers from joining the increasingly popular socialist movement. He not only instituted the Anti-Socialist Law, which forbid both organization by socialists and the circulation of socialist literature, but also enacted social reforms through the first European labour and social laws. In 1883 he enacted the Health Insurance Act, which entitled workers to health insurance at a cost of only two-thirds of the premiums, with employers picking up the other third.[5] A year later he introduced accident insurance and later a pension fund and disability insurance.[6]

Socialism and state welfare programs were two configurational options that arose out of the tensions between competing visions and the interpretation of reality. The socialist's vision was of a classless society while Bismarck's welfare state came out of a view based on a nationalist German unity (and superiority). Against this background pragmatism was just another option in the tension that developed towards the *fin de siècle* and, like most of the others, it too was characterized by some vision of unity. Perhaps ironically, the quest for unity in pragmatism expressed itself as a polemic against the dualistic German idealism rooted in Lutheranism, while the "desires and purposes" of pragmatism arose out of American Calvinism, especially in its congregational tradition.[7] The differences between German Protestantism and American Protestantism have had a tremendous bearing on the development of both political ideology and educational aims and organization. These differences were sensed but not clearly identified by Max Weber, who, in his perception of Calvinism, was trapped by his Lutheranism.[8]

This chapter demonstrates how pragmatism developed as a way to resolve the tensions between specific perceptions of the "conditions to be met" in Dewey's time and the "desires and purposes" of a good life. Using the example of the city of Chicago, I show how the perils of modern industry and metropolis, as they became tangible in the world's most bustling city, were interpreted and opposed in terms of the "desires and purposes." Both sides of the configuration – interpretation of the conditions of life and the "desires and purposes" – were derived from American Protestant visions, ideals, and moral concepts, which had led to an idiosyncratic understanding of democracy. To put it another way: I do not think that pragmatism as a specific mode of thinking or intellectual doctrine could have arisen at that time in, let's say, Lexington, Kentucky; Baton Rouge, Louisiana; Palermo, Sicily; or Ballyshannon, in the Republic of Ireland.[9]

My paper is divided into four sections. In the first section I try briefly to describe the conditions of living in a metropolis such as Chicago and, in a second section, I reconstruct the way many people assessed these conditions as problematic and show how they responded by propagating educational concepts. In the third section, I show how Dewey began to think about contem-

porary phenomena in Ann Arbor, Michigan, and why and how
he changed his analysis in Chicago in 1894. In the fourth
section I analyze his educational theory. I conclude with a short
summary of this chapter.

CHICAGO AT THE *FIN DE SIÈCLE*:
THE PERILS OF METROPOLIS

It is not possible to prove that Chicago was *the* place where the
phenomena of metropolis were most omni-present and tangible,
but we do have data that show how dramatically life conditions
were changing at the edge of Lake Michigan during the fifty
years between 1850 and 1900. We see this when we look at how
much the population of Chicago grew during this time:[10]

1840:	4,470	1890:	1,099,850
1850:	29,963	1900:	1,698,575
1860:	102,260	1910:	2,185,283
1870:	298,977	1920:	2,701,705
1880:	503,185	1930:	3,376,438

Within these ninety years the population increased 800 times.
Within ten years, between 1880 and 1890, it doubled, and
within the next twenty years, between 1890 and 1910, it
doubled again. City government or companies trying to cope
with these numbers in terms of infrastructure — road construction, electricity, transportation, food supply, education, and so
on, not to mention trying to deal with ethnic and cultural differences and communication problems – faced a tremendous
task. But the metropolis not only grew quantitatively: *life*
changed totally. While in 1840 most of Chicago's 4,000 inhab-
itants made a living by farming, trading, or running small enterprises, after 1860 the steel and meat industries began to dominate economic life, as Chicago became the centre of the railroad
system.[11] Among the large integrated steel works were Union

Mill, founded in 1863, US Steel South Works, 1881, Acme Steel, 1907, and US Steel, in Gary, Indiana, 1908. At the peak, about 200,000 people in Chicago were employed in the steel mills and other industries related to steel.[12] During the Civil War Chicago became not only the hub of the American railroad system but also the "Porkopolis" of the United States.[13] The Union Stock Yard opened in 1865 and became the centre of meatpacking in the United States: from 1893 onwards there was no year in which fewer than 15 million head of livestock were unloaded at the stockyards, then slaughtered, packed, and shipped – mostly to the big cities on the East Coast – 50,000 head of livestock a day.[14] Ironically, the Great Fire of 1871, which destroyed the homes of almost a third of Chicago's population, can be seen as a new driving force in generating even more development;[15] for example, financial men such as Henry Greenebaum spread out through the Western world to successfully promote investment in the destroyed city.[16]

Economic developments such as those in Chicago led to unequal distribution of profit. Wealth – the contrast to the poverty often described by concerned contemporaries – became tangible along the shores of Lake Michigan: the first skyscraper, initiated in 1885, was the Home Insurance Building on Addams Street, which had a fireproof metal frame. The Masonic Temple, with twenty-one stories, followed in 1892 and the Tower Building in 1899.[17] After the fire of 1871 the destroyed hotels were rebuilt, the Grand Pacific Hotel in 1872, then the Palmer House, the Tremont, and the Sherman House, all adopting the commercial palazzo style of architecture, all fireproofed and boasting grand lobbies, monumental staircases, elegant parlors, cafes, ballrooms, and so on.[18] For private residences architects such as Frank Lloyd Wright developed a style of their own, blending different impulses in architecture. How much modern architecture reflected the self-confidence of the privileged classes of society[19] can be seen in the proudly presented, monumental 1909 *Plan of Chicago* drawn up by the former director

of works for the World's Columbian Exposition (also called the
Chicago World's Fair).[20]

Entertainment also began to fragment along class lines and
added to the separation of classes.[21] The large population of
immigrants – in 1890, three-quarters of Chicago's residents
claimed foreign-born parentage – enjoyed neither safe housing,
Hautevolee's French cuisine, dignified work, or sanitary conditions. Contemporary life in the stockyards was described by
muckraker journalist and socialist Upton Sinclair in his famous
novel *The Jungle*, published in 1906. In this fictitious report
Sinclair shows that corruption was endemic, helpless people
were exploited, and their humiliation became a "normal" part
of life in this big city. *The Jungle* tells the story of a Lithuanian
immigrant family whose American dream turns into a night-
mare, not because of ill fortune or contretemps but as a result
of thoroughly corrupt conditions created by the privileged.
Crime, alcohol, and prostitution are shown as consequences of
life conditions among the lower classes. How ready the contemporary audience was to read stories like this is apparent
from its sales figures: within a year of publication *The Jungle*
had sold more than 100,000 copies and caused the debates that
led to the 1906 Pure Food and Drug Act and the Meat Inspec-
tion Act.

Sinclair's account was, certainly, exaggerated and polemic.
However, in many respects the story described facts of city life
that were easily observable and thus (somewhat) well known.
Countless bars and saloons had opened,[22] nightclubs had been
founded, and prostitution flourished; by 1900, the Levee, bor-
dered by 18th and 22nd Streets, "was one of the nation's most
infamous sex districts."[23] Chicago became famous for the
"commercialization of sex." This was bemoaned, among other
complaints, in Robert O. Harland's 1912 *The Vice Bondage of
a Great City; or, The Wickedest City in the World the Reign of
Vice, Graft and Political Corruption.*[24] Publications like these
consolidated the impression that life in Chicago and other big

cities at the *fin de siècle* was extremely difficult for most of their residents. This was certainly true for thousands of young children and young people, unsupervised by their hard-working parents, often themselves earning money at risky jobs. Concern for the welfare of workers triggered a Protestant, urban, moral-awakening movement that pointed to the moral decay of the cities.[25] In New York City, Presbyterian minister Charles Henry Parkhurst accused officials of corruption and of being responsible for alcohol abuse and prostitution. In Chicago it was the son of a congregational minister, William Thomas Stead, who led the moral crusade against the conditions of city life through books like *If Christ Came to Chicago*.[26] The famous book *In his Steps* by Congregationalist minister Charles Monroe Sheldon[27] demanded of tens of thousands of middle-class Protestants, "What would Jesus do?" This became a popular slogan with Jesus presented as a moral example rather than a saviour figure.

THE METROPOLIS, ITS PERILS, AND THE EDUCATIONAL REFLEX

From psychology we are aware of the popular illustration of the half-empty or half-full bottle. One aim of psychotherapy is to find ways in which the personality of a person can be strengthened to the point that he or she will reverse his or her interpretation of the bottle from half-empty to half-full. The same alternation in perception can be applied to Chicago. In 1900 there were people who described it as a booming city with the first skyscrapers, sophisticated hotels, cultivated entertaining, and a residential architecture. However, there were also people who saw the "same" Chicago as primarily a city of exploitation, humiliation, and corruption. Descriptions of the social and economic conditions in Chicago provoked broad indignation and disgust. In the eyes of many people, the metropolis had become an overwhelming moral and political problem.[28] Children, young people, and women were believed to be particularly defenceless when exposed to these corrupting conditions and were thus in danger of multiplying the vices of the metropolis. In the words of Congregational minister and penologist Enoch Cobb Wines, children in the cities were virtually "born to crime, brought up for it," and Wines' simple conclusion was: "They must be saved."[29] The children, however, did not respond as expected: when one of Chicago's child labour inspectors, Helen Todd, asked some five hundred children between the ages of fourteen and sixteen whether they would rather attend school if their parents had enough money, more than eighty percent said they preferred the factory over the school; when children in Milwaukee were asked whether they would return to school if they got the same seventy-five cents a day that they earned at menial jobs, only sixteen out of eight thousand youths would have accepted this offer.[30] For many concerned people, these answers were not an expression of young people taking responsibility for work and earning their keep but were seen as an expression of the corrupting influence of the city in general and bad schooling in particular. Young women seemed to be especially at risk, since they had "to face the serious moral problems forced upon them by the reorganization of their sphere of life through its invasion by modern industry."[31] They had to survive by whatever means they could, but they also had to avoid entanglement with the legal system and jail – a dilemma that was not always solved successfully. And even in the case of prison sentences the worries about the young and women prevailed, as reflected in the differentiation of jails into specific sections for women and juveniles.[32]

There was a widely held contemporary view that the city was a breeding ground for injustice, corruption, vices, and crime. There was also a belief that a good education would decrease the problems. In 1899, John Dewey had explained to a Chicago audience that prevailing socio-economic conditions required an educational response.[33] Unlike many European theorists Dewey did not try to ignore the conditions of metropolis but sought to deal with them. "It is silly and futile to ignore and deny economic facts," Dewey stated in 1927. "They do not cease to operate because we refuse to note them, or because we smear them over with sentimental idealizations."[34]

The movement to react towards perceived problems by means of education can be called an 'educationalization' of social problems. In this view, the cure for social deficiencies is enhanced education. This phenomenon was not new at the *fin de siècle* in 1900 but resulted from specific theories developed in the eighteenth century, when the dramatic changes in the developing market economy evoked public criticism about the devastating effects of economic development. These educational reactions resulted from a combination of classical republican and Protestant thinking. Classical republican thinking, with its agricultural orientation, feared the effects of commerce on the soul of man. He would be captivated by the market, would become selfishly pre-occupied with his private fortune, and would forget the common good. This perception of the soul as defenceless in the face of the market – unprotected by any institution – is also typical of Protestant thinking. In contrast, the Catholic faith refers on principle to the Holy Mother Church as providing the opportunity for protection and salvation. While the Catholic's had confession, the Protestant solution to facing the dangers of life was to strengthen the soul of the young in order to protect them from the corrupting temptations of commerce, wealth, and power.[35] It was this Protestant educational paradigm that promised to provide a way to successfully and enduringly secure the world from the possible dangers of modernity. Since then, ideas of progress and concepts of education have been closely connected; questions about the future or progress have been, in almost a reflex reaction, connected with education.[36]

While this reflex of educationalizing social problems was successful – in the sense that it was adapted by different denominations and ideologies other than Protestantism – the specific educational concepts that were developed differed across the denominations. A rather legal approach was initiated in an Anglican context, as the example of Edgar Gardner Murphy shows. In 1904 Murphy, a priest of the Episcopal Church, founded the National Child Labor Committee. Their attempt to protect the young from exploitation in the workplace was incorporated in 1907 into an Act of Congress that had as its mission "promoting the rights, awareness, dignity, well-being, and education of children and youth as they relate to work and working."[37] The juvenile court movement in Chicago in the 1890s[38] also emerged within this denominational context; it was based on "recognition of the obligation of the great mother state to her neglected and erring children, and her obligation to deal with them as children, and wards, rather than to class them as criminals and drive them by harsh measures into the ranks of vice and crime."[39]

Protestant concepts of educationalizing differed considerably from these rather formal solutions; while they kept the idea that, rather than solving problems institutionally, children's souls had to be addressed more directly, by, for instance, teaching them Christian (Protestant) values, preferably in settings that were supposed to be pure, such as the countryside. As early as 1872 we find the example of Congregational minister Charles Loring Brace, who advocated that city children should benefit from exposure to country life.[40] Baptist pastor and later professor of sociology at the University of Chicago Charles Richmond Henderson directed social research projects, including new methods of social investigation such as social surveys and statistical analysis, in order to discover paths out of poverty, which was still seen as an individual failing.[41] Protestant clergyman Josiah Strong, as one of the founders of the Social Gospel Movement, reminded Protestants of the problems of the city and the ultimate need for Christian action.[42] The Social Gospel Movement was supported by prominent members of the new social and economical sciences, such as Richard J. Ely[43] or Henry Carter Adams.[44] Its leader in Chicago, Graham Taylor, the founder and director of Chicago Commons Settlement House and also theology professor of "Biblical Sociology" in the Department of Sociology at Chicago Theological Seminary, defined religion in social action in the context of challenges of the new American frontier, the social frontiers.[45] In this context we should include the activities of Congregational Church Minister George Davies Herron (1893) and the critic of the traditional social welfare of charity Calvinist Robert Archey Woods (1898), who, by collecting shocking data about young working girls,[46] had an important impact on the development of the settlement movement in the United States. By 1911 there were 413 single settlements,[47] among which, of course, Jane Addams' Hull House in Chicago[48] and Graham Taylor's Chicago Commons played a key role.[49] Addams also had an equally important impact on John Dewey's intellectual development.

JOHN DEWEY:
FROM MARXISM TO PROTESTANT DEMOCRACY

Economic developments and their social impacts, most apparent in big cities, had shocked many middle-class Americans, among whom were a noticeably large number of Protestants.[50] Like many other Pragmatists, John Dewey came from a pious Protestant family and shared their concerns about the situation in the US towards the end of the century. As a trained philosopher specializing in German idealism, Dewey began his investigation of how to deal with the causes and effects of modern industry by reading – in this case European socialist literature. As early as 1886, while still in quiet Ann Arbor, Dewey analyzed the changes within industrial society by sympathizing with socialist literature, as we learn from a letter to his wife Alice Chipman: "This morning I spent in the laboratory (*lapsus calami* – I mean library) trying to find something on the effects

of machinery, and woe be to me, I found so much I wished I
hadn't found any. I found a number of French and German his-
tories of laboring class that I didn't know anything about
before."[51] A few days later, he tells her: "My forenoons now are
spent in the library reading up on machinery & wages &c. ... It
has opened up a new field to me. I almost wish sometimes I was
in pol[itical] ec[onomy], it is so thoroughly human."[52] The
socialist interpretation of the world and its material history
seemed to Dewey to provide a way to explain the struggle of the
Western civilization.

Socialist interpretations of the history and the conditions of
life were not unknown in the United States. One of the leaders
of the Social Gospel Movement, Richard T. Ely, had discussed
models of European socialism.[53] Some activists, frustrated by
the ineffectiveness of their social and political activities and by
the political corruption they saw in society, converted to socialism. Among these was Eugene Debs, the leader of the American
Railway Union in Chicago. Debs had been sentenced to a year
in jail for having violated the injunction against the Pullman
strike (1894) and while incarcerated began to read Karl Marx.
In his retrospective writing on this period he says:

> The Chicago strike was in many respects the grandest indus-
> trial battle in history, and I am prouder of my small share in
> it than of any other act of my life. Men, women and chil-
> dren were on the verge of starvation at the "model city" of
> Pullman ... President Cleveland says that we were put down
> because we had acted in violation of the Sherman Anti-Trust
> law of 1890. Will he kindly state what other trusts were
> proceeded against and what capitalists were sentenced to
> prison during his administration?[54]

It is interesting to see what happened when Dewey moved
from Ann Arbor to Chicago in 1894. His move put him right
in the middle of the Pullman Strike, the most sensational of all

of the 20,783 workers' strikes reported to the police in a period of only twenty years (1881–1900).[55] Fired up by the events, Dewey went to see Jane Addams and they discussed how social, economical, and political conditions could and should be understood and changed in order to avoid desperation and strikes. As they talked, Dewey apparently took the view that antagonism between the labour class and capitalists was inevitable in a capitalist society – a testimony to his reading in Ann Arbor. As he wrote in a letter to his wife, Addams did not disagree with the feeling of injustice but with Dewey's idea of the necessity of antagonism. She had explained to him "that antagonism was not only useless and harmful, but entirely unnecessary; that it lay never in the objective differences, which would always grow into unity if left alone." Dewey (at first) did not agree at all with this characterization, as he told his wife in the same letter, for he defended the idea of the inevitable difference of the classes. But, waking that same night, Dewey took up the letter again and now wrote: "I guess I'll have to give it all up & start over again. I suppose that's the subjective nature of sin; the only reality is unity, but we assume there is antagonism & then it all goes wrong."[56] Two days later he apologized to Addams: "I wish to take back what I said the other night. Not only is actual antagonizing bad, but the assumption that there is or may be antagonism is bad."[57] The original dualistic worldview that Dewey had sympathized with while reading European literature on labour classes in Ann Arbor had vanished. Jane Addams had given him an interpretation of the situation that was much better suited to his disgust with the conditions of life in the big cities than the ideas of dualisms and antagonism between classes. This interpretation encouraged the idea of the original unity that had been deformed by modern developments.

Marxism or socialism believes that unity will occur *after* the antagonism between classes and the revolution by the masses (which will give rise to the ideal of the classless society), but

Dewey realized that even the interpretation of reality as antagonistic is an intellectual mistake or, as he puts it, a "sin." He did not give up his ideal of unity – far from it – but he abandoned the idea that only antagonism would lead to this unity. Unity became not an aim apart from a means but a real and normal condition of life, and any kind of antagonism was seen as a deviation from normality. The real antagonisms in the life of the metropolis were not to be overcome through the practical consequences of the intellectual tools provided by historical materialism but instead by the practical consequences of democracy, which Dewey had come to believe was the final form of social and political life, the form that human evolution had been leading toward.

It is quite characteristic that Dewey and his pragmatist colleagues did not see the sciences, technology, or industry as the source of the misery in the cities. They shared the common American belief that the democratic foundation of the United States had made its impressive developments possible and that democracy had also affected the progress of technology. The latter idea was clear in statements made at the celebration of the opening of the Erie Canal in 1825: the Canal was the "proof" that "will present to all mankind of the capabilities of a free people, whose energies, undirected by absolute authority, have accomplished, with a sum insufficient to support regal pomp for a single year, a work of greater public utility, than the congregated forces of Kings have effected since the foundations of the earth."[58]

The problem the pragmatists had with modernity was that the inverse of this process – the reinforcement of democracy by technology and industry – had not occurred in the late nineteenth century. In this context the idea of intelligent adaption gained in prominence. On this interpretation eighteenth-century democracy, the primary basis of modernization, had not kept pace with social transformations caused by industry[59] and thus had not developed into an industrial democracy. This failure to adapt was believed to have resulted from the influence of a dualistic philosophy that had originated in slave societies[60] and educational ideas that had been developed in non-democratic societies. As a result, philosophy and education would have to be reconstructed. [61] The seminal step in this reconstruction was to emancipate philosophy from the constraints of a dualistic philosophy dating back to the ancient Greek philosophers as well as acknowledging the truth of evolution and the fact that processes change as a result of social interaction, facts determined by modern science, whose methods should now be applied to society. As George Herbert Mead urged: "The modern world by means of this method has made a new heaven and a new earth; it has changed the fixed objects of Aristotle for the process of evolution. By means of this method we shall be able to deal with our social problems, by means of it we are now coming to the place where we can discover the laws of man as a social being, as part of a process."[62]

This new philosophy and educational theory had two interrelated dimensions. First, it was meant to be an important way by which it could be made clear that the conditions of life had become deviant. Second, its clear thinking would foster democracy in industrial society. Democracy was not an alternative to other understandings of associated life but was understood as "idea of community life itself," as Dewey stated in *The Public and Its Problems* in 1927.[63] Consequently, educational concepts had to be a part of this community, which was evolving towards democracy. These educational concepts would contribute to correcting the contemporary conditions of life for children and young people.

THE NEW EDUCATIONAL CONCEPT
IN A (PROTESTANT) DEMOCRACY

Recent studies have shown how deeply pragmatism is rooted in Protestant thinking or mentality[64] and have made clear that the

motive underlying pragmatist thinking and acting was to erect
the Kingdom of God on earth.[65] If intelligent activity is adaptation "of the environment to the individual's needs and ends,
rather than vice versa,"[66] then it is important to see what this
concept looked like when applied to the metropolis. If democracy is the "idea of community life itself" and community
means some form of unity, then "the cure for the ailments of
democracy is more democracy," as Dewey argued in 1927 in
The Public and Its Problems.[67] The previous ideal of rural
community had degenerated in the nineteenth century into a
"Great Society" that had developed in the context of the emergence of modern sciences, industry, telecommunications, and
the metropolis as living space. In the course of these changes
the social classes were seen as having become torn apart and
left with hardly any mutual interaction. This "Great Society"
now needed to change into the "Great Community."[68] In the
tradition of Protestantism, Dewey reminds readers that democracy is *not* to be limited to institutional forms, to "the forms to
which we are accustomed in democratic governments," such as
"general suffrage, elected representatives, majority rule, and so
on."[69] Instead, democracy means unrestricted interaction,
which will have two main results. First, there is the education
effect that will result from developing the individual potential
of every single person and, second, the increased sharing of
individual experiences and knowledge. Under those conditions
the people can develop into a deliberative public, achieving the
ideal of eighteenth-century democracy under the conditions of
modernity. Dewey's religious convictions influenced his view
that this interactive public would, in the end, achieve unity
over chaos or diversity. This belief was illustrated in his significant *A Common Faith*, published only a few years later in
1934.[70]

This vision leads to a very interesting social, ethical, and educational picture. On one hand each individual tries to be part of
the activities of the different groups to which he belongs. By

doing so, he fosters the social, intellectual, and physical capacities that these different groups demand. On the other hand, the groups need the capabilities of the members to be in accordance with the aims of the group if the group is to survive. Now, since all individuals belong to more than one group, this mutual interaction of individual and group, which has its aim the liberation of the potentials of the individual, can only take place if the groups themselves can interact with other groups – for example social classes with other social classes.[71]

Human nature is essentially social, and thus educational, as Mead pointed out in his lectures *Philosophy of Education.* "We know that through necessities of the human family, vagrant man has become attached – has been placed. *The center of this relationship* is not the sexual attachment, *but it centers in the child* – the necessity of permanence, protection, providing, cooperation – and out of these necessities society has arisen."[72] In other words, "education of the child ... takes place in a type of social environment ... And this social environment is of ... capital importance for the development of the child."[73] It is the "social environment" that "determines very largely those differences which we recognize."[74]

This understanding of social environment allows Dewey to make a surprising argument as to why life on the streets and in the criminal gangs of the cities is detrimental. In his seminal work *The Public and Its Problems,* Dewey argues that a member of a gang or a band of robbers will develop those capacities that the group wants, such as stealing, doing a runner, robbing, pick pocketing, lying convincingly, and so on. Dewey's criticism of these learned activities is not so much moral or judicial, at least ostensibly, as it is political and educational. He argues that because robber bands cannot interact flexibly with other social groups such as schools, the church, the Boy Scouts, or sports clubs – in other words because robber bands are isolated from other social groups – the members of these groups develop the abilities desired by the group at the cost of failing to develop potential abilities that would be developed in other groups. Thus children who are part of robber bands or gangs of thieves or who spend their time loitering in the streets of a metropolis will not develop all their potential and will not be able to help to contribute to a public that is the core element of the "Great Community" and of democracy. The perils of the "Great Society" – of metropolis and inhuman capitalism – will then persist.[75] Also in 1923, Mead presented a similar argument: Democracy depends on democratically educated and democratically minded people:

> That is what democratic government means, for the issue does not actually exist as such, until the members of the community realize something of what it means to them individually and collectively. There cannot be self-government until there can be an intelligent will expressed in the community growing out if the intelligent attitudes of the individuals and groups in whose experience the community exists. Our institutions are insofar democratic that when a public sentiment is definitely formed and expressed it is authoritative.[76]

This sentiment is both a condition and a result of education. Some twenty years earlier Dewey had referred to the isolation of individuals and subjects as "waste in education" and postulated an educational organization in which "things" are "getting ... into connection with one another, so that they work easily, flexibly, and fully."[77] For him the family remains the ideal type of educational organization and by generalizing its characteristics "we have the ideal school."[78] Manifold interaction with subjects leads to perpetual interaction and communication:

> The child who has a variety of materials and facts wants to talk about them, and his language becomes more refined and full, because it is controlled and informed by realities.

Reading and writing, as well as the oral use of language, may be taught on this basis. It can be done in a *related* way, as the outgrowth of the child's social desire to recount his experiences and get in return the experiences of others, directed always through contact with the facts and forces which determine the truth communicated.[79]

In other words, the old communities of the agrarian society of the eighteenth century still served as a model – not a political one but an educational one. The reason for the modern crisis was seen in the "dislocation and unsettlement of local communities,"[80] and the solution was education. The American School, modernized, unites the children in a sort of religious act: "Our schools, in bringing together those of different nationalities, languages, traditions and creeds, in assimilating them together upon the basis of what is common and public in endeavor and achievement, are performing the social unity out of which in the end genuine religious unity must grow."[81] For Dewey, the fundamental sense of community life" can only be restored by "face-to-face intercourse."[82] "There is no substitute for the vitality and depth of close and direct intercourse and attachment,"[83] which will, at the same time, redeem democracy. "Democracy must begin at home, and home is the neighborly community."[84]

NOTES

1 Paper presented in the panel "Fin de siècle Social Crisis: Reconstructing the World and the Appeal of Pragmatism" at ISCHE 29, University of Hamburg, 25–28 July 2007.

2 John Dewey, "Adaptation," in *A Cyclopedia of Education* 1, ed. Paul Monroe (New York: Macmillan, 1919), 35.

3 John Dewey, "Accommodation," in *A Cyclopedia of Education* 1, ed. Paul Monroe(New York: Macmillan, 1919), 24f.

4 Dewey, "Adaptation," 35.

5 In contrast the {attempt to introduce} universal health insurance by
   US President Barack Obama in 2009/10 was labeled as socialist in the
   US – exactly what Bismarck wanted to prevent.

6 Lothar Machtan , Ed., *Bismarcks Sozialstaat – Beiträge zur
   Geschichte der Sozialpolitik und zur sozialpolitischen Geschichtss-
   chreibung* (Frankfurt A.M./New York: Campus, 1994).

7 Steven C. Rockefeller, *John Dewey. Religious Faith and Democratic
   Humanism* (New York: Columbia University Press, 1991); Daniel
   Tröhler, "The 'Kingdom of God on Earth' and Early Chicago Prag-
   matism," *Educational Theory 56*, no. 1 (2006): 89–105; Daniel
   Tröhler, "The Educationalization of the Modern World. Progress,
   Passion, and the Protestant Promise of Education," in *The Education-
   alization of Social Problems,* eds. Paul Smeyers and Marc Depaepe
   (Dordrecht: Springer, 2009), 31–46; Daniel Tröhler, "Responding the
   Cultural Construction of Modernity: The Chicago Pragmatism," in
   Pragmatism and Modernities, eds. Daniel Tröhler, Thomas Schlag,
   and Fritz Osterwalder (Rotterdam: Sense, 2010), 21–40.

8 Daniel Tröhler, "Max Weber und die protestantische Ethik in
   Amerika," in *Rationalisierung und Bildung bei Max Weber: Beiträge
   zur Historischen Bildungsforschung,* eds. Jürgen Oelkers, Rita Casale,
   Rebekka Horlacher, and Sabina Larcher Klee (Bad Heilbrunn:
   Klinkhardt, 2006): 111–34.

9 William James (Boston) or Ferdinand Scanning Scott Schiller (first
   Oxford, UK, then Southern California) are of course justly identified
   as pragmatists, too. However, the Chicago pragmatism has its own
   idiosyncrasies, with a strong emphasis on democracy and education.
   It is not by chance that it was William James who came up with the
   label the "Chicago School" to indicate a distinct way of dealing intellectually with social and philosophical problems. See William James,
   "The Chicago School," *Psychological Bulletin 1* (1904): 1–5. It is this
   distinctive Chicago pragmatism that I focus on in this chapter.

10 Thomas Lee Philpott, *The Slum and the Ghetto. Immigrants, Blacks,
   and Reformers in Chicago 1880–1930* (Belmont: Wadsworth Publishing, 1998), 6.

11 The first railroad in Chicago had its maiden journey in 1848. Using the example of Rochester, New York, historian Paul E. Johnson has impressively reconstructed how life in a city could change when the access to a modern transport network such as the Erie Canal was introduced and has shown how these 'capitalist' developments led to a religious revival called the Second Grand Awakening. Paul E. Johnson, *A Shopkeepers Millennium. Society and Revivals in Rochester, New York, 1815–1837* (New York: Hill and Wang, 2004, first edition 1978).

12 David Bensman and Mark R. Wilson, "Iron and Steel," in *The Encyclopedia of Chicago* (Chicago: The University of Chicago Press, 2004), 424ff.

13 Porkopolis was the nickname given the city with largest number of slaughterhouse businesses. Cincinnati was the first city to have this nickname (as early as 1843), which went to Chicago after 1860. Louise Carroll Wade, "Meatpacking," in *The Encyclopedia of Chicago* (Chicago: The University of Chicago Press, 2004), 515f.

14 An impressive view of the rise of Chicago and insights into city conditions is provided by the film "Chicago, City of the Century," co-produced by WGBH Boston and WTTW Chicago in association with the Chicago Historical Society. The film is based on the book *City of the Century: The Epic of Chicago and the Making of America* by Don Miller (New York: Simon and Schuster, 1996; Touchstone, 1997). Wade, "Meatpacking," 515–17.

15 Karen Sawislak, *Smoldering City. Chicagoans and the Great Fire, 1871–1874* (Chicago: The University of Chicago Press, 1995).

16 Ibid., 321.

17 Carl W. Condit, *The Chicago School of Architecture* (Chicago: The University of Chicago Press, 1964).

18 Molly W. Berger, "Hotels," in *The Encyclopedia of Chicago* (Chicago: The University of Chicago Press, 2004), 394.

19 See, for instance, the essays of Montgomery Schuyler in *American Architecture and Other Writings,* eds. William H. Jordy and Ralph Coe (Cambridge, MA: The Belknap Press of Harvard University Press, 1961) and the essays by Henry Van Brunt, *Architecture and Society.*

Selected Essays, in William A. Coles, ed. (Cambridge, MA: The
Belknap Press of Harvard University Press, 1969).

20 Daniel H. Burnham and Edward H. Bennet, *Plan of Chicago, Prepared under the Direction of the Commercial Club* (1909). Newly
edited by Charles Moore (New York: The Da Capo Press, 1970).

21 James Hubert McVicker, *The Press, the Pulpit, and the Stage: A
Lecture Delivered at Central Music Hall,* Chicago, 28 November
1882 (Chicago: Western News Co., 1883); Lewis A. Erenberg,
"Entertaining Chicagoans," in *The Encyclopedia of Chicago*
(Chicago: The University of Chicago Press, 2004), 270ff.

22 Perry R. Duis, *The Saloon. Public Drinking in Chicago and Boston,
1880–1920* (Urbana, IL: University of Illinois Press, 1983).

23 Cynthia M. Blair, "Prostitution," in *The Encyclopedia of Chicago*
(Chicago: The University of Chicago Press, 2004), 651.

24 Robert O. Harland, *The Vice Bondage of a Great City; or, The
Wickedest City in the World the Reign of Vice, Graft and Political
Corruption* (Chicago: Young People's Civic League, 1912).

25 Paul Boyer, *Urban and Moral Order in America 1820–1920* (Cambridge, MA: Harvard University Press, 1978), 162ff.

26 William T. Stead, *If Christ Came to Chicago. A Plea for the Union of
All Who Love in the Service of All Who Suffer* (Chicago: Laird &
Lee, 1894).

27 Charles Monroe Sheldon, *In His Steps: What Would Jesus Do?*
(Chicago: Advance Publishing Co., 1896).

28 Henry George, *Progress and Poverty: An Inquiry into the Cause of
Industrial Depressions, and of Increase of Want with Increase of
Wealth – The Remedy* (San Francisco: W. M. Hinton and Co., 1879);
Jacob A. Riis, *How the Other Half Lives: Studies among the Tene-
ments of New York* (New York: Charles Scribner's Sons, 1890); Ben-
jamin O. Flower, *Civilization's Inferno, or, Studies in the Social Cellar*
(Boston: Arena Publishing Company, 1893); Lincoln Steffens, *The
Shame of the Cities* (New York: McLure, 1904); James Bryce, "The
Menace of Great Cities," in *Housing Problems in America, Proceed-
ings of the Second National Conference on Housing* (New York:
National Housing Association, 1912), 17–22.

29 Quoted in Anthony M. Platt, *The Child Savers. The Inventions of Delinquency* (Chicago: The University of Chicago Press, 1969), vi.

30 Helen M. Todd, "Why Children Work: The Children's Answer," *McClure's Magazine* 6 (April, 1913): 68–79; David Tyack, *Seeking Common Ground. Public Schools in a Diverse Society* (Cambridge, MA: Harvard University Press, 2003), 98ff.

31 Robert A. Woods and Albert J. Kennedy, *Young Working Girls. A Summary from Two Thousand Social Workers* (Boston: Houghton Mifflin Company, 1913), 1f.

32 Jess Maghan, "Jails and Prisons," in *The Encyclopedia of Chicago* (Chicago: The University of Chicago Press, 2004), 432.

33 John Dewey, "The School and Social Progress," in *John Dewey: The Middle Works, Vol. 1* (Carbondale, IL: Southern Illinois University Press, 1976)(Original 1899), 6ff.

34 John Dewey, *The Public and Its Problems* (Athens: Ohio University Press, 1954) (first edition 1927), 156.

35. Daniel Tröhler, "History and Historiography of Education. Some Remarks on the Utility of Historical Knowledge in the Age of Efficiency," *Encounters on Education/Encuentros sobre Educación/Rencontres sur l'Éducation* 7 (2006): 5–24.

36 Tröhler, "The Educationalization of the Modern World."

37 See http://www.nationalchildlabor.org/ (accessed 12 July 2007).

38 Elisabeth J. Clapp, *The Chicago Juvenile Court Movement in the 1890s* (1995) http://www.le.ac.uk/hi/teaching/papers/clapp1.html#fn1 (accessed 12 July 2007).

39 Hastings H. Hart, "Distinctive Features of the Juvenile Court," in *Annals of the American Academy of Political and Social Science* 36 (1910): 60.

40 Charles Loring Brace, *The Dangerous Classes of New York and Twenty Years' Work Among Them* (New York: Wynkoop and Hallenbeck, 1872).

41 Charles Richmond Henderson, *The Social Spirit in America* (Meadville, PA / New York: Flood and Vincent, 1897); Charles Richmond Henderson, *Social Settlements* (New York: Lentilhon, 1899); Charles Richmond Henderson, *Modern Prison Systems: Their Orga-*

nization and Regulation in Various Countries of Europe and America
(Washington: Govt. Print. Office, 1903).

42 Josiah Strong, *Our Country: Its Possible Future and Its Present Crisis*
(New York: The American Home Missionary Society, 1885); Josiah
Strong, *The Challenge of the City* (New York: Young People's Mis-
sionary Movement, 1907).

43 Richard J. Ely, *The Social Aspects of Christianity and Other Essays*
(New York: Thomas Y. Crowell, 1889).

44 Henry C. Adams, *Relation of the State to Industrial Action* (Balti-
more: American Economic Association, 1887).

45 Graham Taylor, *Religion in Social Action* (New York: Dodd, Mead
and Company, 1913); Graham Taylor, *Pioneering on Social Frontiers*
(Chicago: The University of Chicago Press, 1930); Graham Taylor,
Through Forty Years (Chicago: Chicago Commons Association,
1936); see also Louise Carroll Wade, *Graham Taylor. Pioneer for
Social Justice, 1851–1938* (Chicago: The University of Chicago Press,
1964).

46 Woods and Kennedy, *Young Working Girls.*

47 Robert A. Woods and Albert J. Kennedy, *Handbook of Settlements*
(New York: Charities Publication Committee, 1911).

48 Daniel Tröhler, "Modern City, Social Justice, and Education. Early
Pragmatism as Exemplified by Jane Addams," in *Education and
Pragmatism,* eds. Daniel Tröhler and Jürgen Oelkers (Rotterdam:
Sense Publishers, 2005), 69–93.

49 Jane Addams, *The Spirit of Youth and the City Streets* (New York:
Macmillan, 1909); Taylor, *Through Forty Years.*

50 Boyer, *Urban and Moral Order in America 1820–1920.*

51 John Dewey, Letter to Alice Chipman Dewey, dated 29 March 1886
in L. Hickman (electronic ed.), The Correspondence of John Dewey
(Nr. 00033). Retrieved from InteLex Past Masters Database: The
Correspondence of John Dewey. (Charlottesville, VA: InteLex
Corporation).

52 John Dewey, Letter to Alice Chipman Dewey, dated 1 April 1886.
In L. Hickman (electronic ed.), The Correspondence of John Dewey
(Nr. 00039). Retrieved from InteLex Past Masters Database: The

Correspondence of John Dewey. (Charlottesville, VA: InteLex Corporation).

53 Richard J. Ely, *French and German Socialism in Modern Times* (New York: Harper and Brothers, 1883).

54 Eugene V. Debs, *Debs: His Life, Writings and Speeches: with a Department of Appreciations* (Girard, Kan.: *The Appeal to Reason* 1908), 204f.

55 Illinois Bureau of Labor Statistics, 1902, 496–500.

56 John Dewey, Letter to Alice Chipman Dewey dated 10 October 1894. In L. Hickman (electronic ed.), The Correspondence of John Dewey (Nr. 00206). Retrieved from InteLex Past Masters Database: The Correspondence of John Dewey. (Charlottesville, VA: InteLex Corporation).

57 John Dewey, Letter to Jane Addams dated 12 October 1894. In L. Hickman (electronic ed.), The Correspondence of John Dewey (Nr. 00619). Retrieved from InteLex Past Masters Database: The Correspondence of John Dewey. (Charlottesville, VA: InteLex Corporation).

58 Quoted in David E. Nye, *American Technological Sublime* (Cambridge, MA: MIT Press, 1994, 36). In contrast to most of the European intelligentsia, the Americans had little doubt about the harmony of nature and industry. As one of the great heroes in American poetry, Ralph Waldo Emerson said: "Readers of poetry see the factory-village, and the railway, and fancy that the poetry of the landscape is broken up by these; ... but the poet sees them fall within the great Order not less than the bee-hive, or the spider's geometric web. Nature adopts them very fast into her vital circles, and the gliding train of cars she loves like her own" (Emerson 1844, cited in Julie Wosk, *Breaking Frame. Technology and the Visual Arts in the Nineteenth Century* (Piscataway, NJ: Rutgers University Press, 1992). For how much Dewey respected Emerson as a democratic thinker, see John Dewey, "Emerson, the Philosopher of Democracy," in *John Dewey: The Middle Works, Vol. 3* (Carbondale: Southern Illinois University Press, 1977, original 1903).

59 John Dewey, "The Social-Economic Situation and Education," in

John Dewey: The Later Works, Vol. 8 (Carbondale: Southern Illinois University Press, 1986, original 1933), 55, 59.

60 John Dewey, *The Quest for Certainty: A Study of the Relation of Knowledge and Action* (London: George Allen & Unwin, 1930).

61 John Dewey, "What I Believe," in *John Dewey: The Later Works, Vol. 5*, (Carbondale: Southern Illinois University Press, 1984, original 1930), 277; Dewey, "The Social-Economic Situation and Education," *John Dewey: The Later Works, Vol. 8* (Carbondale: Southern Illinois University Press, 1986, original 1933), 43–76.

62 George Herbert Mead, *Philosophy of Education*, edited and introduced by Gert Biesta and Daniel Tröhler (Boulder: Paradigm Publishers, 2008, original typescript 1910), 150.

63 Dewey, *The Public and Its Problems*, 148.

64 Bruce Kuklick, *Churchmen and Philosophers from Jonathan Edwards to John Dewey* (New Haven: Yale University Press, 1985); Rockefeller, *John Dewey*.

65 Tröhler, "The 'Kingdom of God on Earth'."

66 Dewey, "Adaptation," 35.

67 Dewey, *The Public and Its Problems*, 146.

68 Ibid., 143ff.

69 Ibid., 144.

70 John Dewey, "A Common Faith," in *John Dewey: The Later Works, Vol. 14* (Carbondale: Southern Illinois University Press, 1986) (original 1934).

71 Ibid., 147f.

72 Mead, *Philosophy of Education*, 23.

73 Ibid., 31.

74 Ibid.

75 Dewey, *The Public and Its Problems*, 147.

76 George Herbert Mead, "Scientific Method and the Moral Sciences," in *George Herbert Mead, Selected Writings*, ed. Andrew J. Reck (Chicago: University of Chicago Press, 1964, original 1923), 257f.

77 John Dewey, "The School and Society," in *John Dewey: The Middle Works, Vol. 1* (Carbondale: Southern Illinois Press, 1976) (original 1899), 39.

78 Ibid., 24.

79 Ibid., 35.

80 Dewey, *The Public and Its Problems*, 147.

81 John Dewey, "Religion and Our Schools," in *John Dewey: The Middle Works, Vol. 4* (Carbondale: Southern Illinois University Press, 1977, original 1908), 175.

82 Dewey, *The Public and Its Problems*, 212.

83 Ibid., 213.

84 Ibid.

2

Must Democratic Aims and Means Ally?
A Historical-Philosophical Answer from an Unlikely Context

JAMES SCOTT JOHNSTON

INTRODUCTION

I begin this chapter with a political statement. The arrangement of democratic practices is an ongoing issue in educational theory, to judge by the amount of attention given in comparative and international education to the effects of globalization. Getting the right balance between cultural sensitivity on the one hand and viable programs to uphold social, personal, and institutional freedoms and responsibilities on the other is extremely difficult and contentious. Obviously, few openly wish for educational programs and practices that ride roughshod over the cultural sensibilities of those to whom the educational programs are directed. Yet, there is a very good chance that this is just what may happen if attention is not paid to prevailing social and cultural practices. The failures evidenced by the history of post-colonial attempts to import various democratic practices while also constructing spaces for democratic choices testifies to this.

The importance of creating local spaces for legitimate, democratic, educational practice is only now being realized.[1] Past attempts at carving out democratic practices in the post-colonial context often ended in violent uprisings (Zimbabwe, Algeria, and the Democratic Republic of Congo), the maintenance of otherwise oppressive regimes (South Africa), severe penury (Chad, Ethiopia, Eritrea), or some combination of all of these. More recent attempts to redress past injustices and provide for democratic spaces have only marginally improved matters for many of these nations and international bodies continue to wrangle over nation-states' responsibilities in light of these experiences. My point is not to engage in a debate on international politics. It is rather to remind us that the local spaces required for democratic practices are often underdeveloped. It is these spaces, I would argue, that must be at the forefront of any democratic, institutional change.

While we cannot condone the practice of drawing historical rules from particular events, we can make the claim that certain elements need to be in place in order for the possibility of local, democratic spaces. We can say, for example, that issues involving cultural 'dissonance' or 'disconnect' must be addressed. Often this is done with input from local community members who have a (large) hand in crafting educational policy. There also needs to be sensitivity on the part of all involved to certain social and cultural practices that require attention in designing various programs. As well, democratic procedures for public participation in the decision-making processes are necessary.

Each of these is important, yet nowhere near enough. I want to suggest that we must dig much deeper into what constitutes local, democratic practices, with the aid of John Dewey's discussion of the historical situation in China during the May 4th movement. Particular issues that developed out of Dewey's understanding of and interaction with Chinese scholars and Chinese culture, economics, and politics are instructive.[2] The contexts of Chinese civilization, particularly the religious/philosophical Confucian tradition, with its attendant rules and practices for living, are fore-grounded. This is necessary because any reconstruction of culture and cultural practices requires that the point of departure be taken from already existent customs, values, and beliefs. Configurations of local, democratic practice must develop out of prior configurations if they are to be legitimated.

It is not an exaggeration to say that Dewey saw the May 4th movement in China as providing the first real opportunity for genuine democratic practice in over two millennia. For the first time, students, scholars, and the learned public were at one in their insistence on ground-up transformation of social and cultural institutions. The important term to emphasize here is 'ground-up.' Dewey saw the potential for democracy and democratic practices as greater in China than in any other nation in Asia (and a few in Western Europe), precisely because he saw the spirit of democracy reflected in the wills of local scholars and members of the lay, educated public. The movement was not one from without – this was not, in Dewey's estimation at least, a case of exported democracy. This nascent democratic spirit was home-grown. From the fall of the Q'ing Dynasty, the development of the First Republic in 1911, and the subsequent student uprising and unrest that constituted the first rumblings of what would become the May 4th movement, Dewey sensed the opportunity for a democracy in spirit. This was a spirit that would overcome ancient traditions not by casting them aside, or violently ploughing them under (as in the Cultural Revolution of the 1960s), but rather by taking them as a point of departure for the development of a literate, informed, and inquiring public, able to make its own decisions from its own contexts.

CONFIGURING DEMOCRACY: DEMOCRATIC ENDS THROUGH DEMOCRATIC MEANS

Undoubtedly, the text that best provides a cogent and succinct exposition of John Dewey's conception of democracy is *Democracy and Education*. There, Dewey says:

A democracy is more than a form of government; it is primarily a mode of associated living, of conjoint communicated experience. The extension in space of the number of individuals who participate in an interest so that each has to refer his own action to that of others, and to consider the action of others to give point and direction to his own, is equivalent to the breaking down of those barriers of class, race, and national territory which kept men from perceiving the full import of their activity. These more numerous and more varied points of contact denote a greater diversity of stimuli to which an individual has to respond; they consequently put a premium on variation in his action. They secure a liberation of powers which remain suppressed as long as the incitations to action are partial, as they must be in a group which in its exclusiveness shuts out many interests.[3]

Speaking of a specifically democratic inquiry, an inquiry that would proceed on a democratic basis, Dewey says, "We cannot set up, out of our heads, something we regard as an ideal society. We must base our conception upon societies which actually exist, in order to have any assurance that our ideal is a practicable one. But ... the ideal cannot simply repeat the traits which are actually found. *The problem is to extract the desirable traits of forms of community life which actually exist, and employ them to criticize undesirable features and suggest improvement.*"[4]

Democracy in Dewey's estimation is not a procedural or legal affair, though it does enfold these; rather, it is a way of living – an associated, communicative living – in which a reciprocal referral of (one's) human conduct to the conduct of others is central.[5] Beyond this, the passage suggests that one's life is enriched as one dismantles obstacles to communication. I wish to focus on the obstacles. Dewey mentions class, race, and national territory in the above passage, and this list suggests

that nationalism (or, in any event, national hostilities) is a
target. However, we must be careful. If national territory is to
be dismantled, what means should be employed? It is not
enough to suggest, "by non-violent means." For one thing,
what constitutes violence obviously cannot be limited to physical coercion. The violence that is done to cultures and publics
through occupation, colonization, and unfair trade practices is
as contestable as other invasive manoeuvres. If the dismantling
of national territory involves these practices, it confounds its
own ends. What I am driving at here is the need for democratic
ends and democratic means to operate simultaneously. One can
no more insist on democracy (or democratic practices) after colonization than after a full-scale invasion. Consistency must be
manifest throughout.

Dewey makes his case for consistency quite clear in *Freedom
and Culture*. There, speaking of authoritarian governments,
Dewey claims,

> If there is one conclusion to which human experience
> unmistakably points it is that democratic ends demand dem-
> ocratic methods for their realization ... Our first defence
> [against authoritarianism] is to realize that democracy can
> be served only by the slow day by day adoption and conta-
> gious diffusion in every phase of our common life of
> methods that are identical with the ends to be reached and
> that recourse to monistic, wholesale, absolutist procedures is
> a betrayal of human freedom no matter in what guise it
> presents itself.[6]

Clearly, there is no question about Dewey's rhetoric regarding
democratic ends and means. Nevertheless, does Dewey's
"theory" of democracy embrace what Dewey thinks is central?
Elsewhere, I maintain that the best way to understand democracy (for Dewey) is to see it as a process or method: a process
in which growth, of the individual and of the group, commu-

nity, and society, is augmented.[7] I shall briefly discuss my thesis here and then turn to the question of how this plays out in democratic education in the context of democratic ends and means.

In the conception of democracy I envision, growth is the terminal event. Dewey says in *Experience and Nature*: "The reality is the growth-process itself; childhood and adulthood are phases of a continuity, in which just because it is a history, the later cannot exist until the earlier exists ... and in which the later makes use of the registered and cumulative outcome of the earlier – or, more strictly, is its utilization."[8]

What, then, is meant by growth? Here is Dewey discussing growth in *Experience and Education*: "Growth, or growing and developing, not only physically but intellectually and morally, is one exemplification of the principle of continuity."[9] I have suggested elsewhere that growth is closely bound to experience – to the satisfaction found in certain generic traits of existence. These traits are "qualitative individuality and constant relations, contingency and need, movement and arrest ... This fact is source both of values and of their precariousness; both of immediate possession which is causal and of reflection with is a precondition of the secure attainment and appropriation. Any theory that detects and defines these traits is therefore but a ground-map of the province of criticism, establishing base lines to be employed in more intricate triangulations."[10] According to Dewey, the manifestation of these traits is the springboard for meaningful relations, including interpersonal and social relations. Put simply, we engage in mutually growth-producing experiences. Moreover, this becomes the basis for social groups.

Banding together in larger groups (communities) affords persons the opportunity to minimize 'bad' experiences (problems or concerns) in favour of 'good' experiences (those that heighten the generic traits of existence). Eventually, communities form bridges to one another as shared problems or concerns are found, investigated, and remedied. The process or means of this finding, investigation, and remedy is inquiry. Inquiry, I argue, is the central means to growth, both individual and social. Democracy is inquiry formalized to meet the needs and solve the problems of communities through the development of institutions and procedures that help maximize peoples' good experiences and minimize their bad ones. Democracy is located not so much in the institutions that serve people (though this is necessary) as in the process of solving problems and augmenting experiences. Dewey is clear about this in the foregoing passage from *Democracy and Education*.

Education is the means by which this inquiry is developed, as well as the social wherewithal to solve problems and develop social skills and habits. Inquiry is a social means to an experiential end and as such has its terminus in a satisfactory experience. Inquiry that fails to result in a problem solved, or a satisfactory experience, is re-tooled. There is no "one method" of inquiry, though there are techniques that have been successful for a wide range of problems. The chief function of the school is to provide children with opportunities to develop this inquiry. In the elementary grades, such inquiry will be closely allied to activities of daily living and is necessarily informal. As the child ages and progresses through the grades, inquiry becomes more formalized and complex. Nevertheless, the point of inquiry is the same throughout.

Inquiry must be democratic. It is the means to growth and if it is undemocratic, if it coasts on fixed principles or absolutes, it will not achieve a democratic outcome. Indeed, it has the potential to become a terrible weapon in the hands of tyrants and dictators, as the twentieth century can attest. What makes inquiry democratic is not the ends to which it is put (which, in any event, must *ex hypothesi* be democratic) but rather the means by which it is practiced. *Democratic inquiry is a flexible, non-authoritarian, experimental approach to solving problems of human conduct and associated living.* Democratic inquiry stresses the importance of problem-solving: inquiry must end in a meaningful state of affairs for it to be complete. Another way to put this is that inquiry must be operationalized. Democratic inquiry in educational settings is operationalized when children develop and practice "habits" of inquiring into various subject matters and then carry this inquiring in their daily lives on well past school.

Dewey does not focus on the various ways in which people are silenced in communicative encounters.[11] However, he certainly would lament such silencing. Barriers to progress (which in this case is understood as problem finding, investigation, experimentation, and evaluation, together with the solution to the problem) are discouraged. If inquiry must be carried out in such a manner that only some people are privy to certain information, or there are arbitrary or one-sided limits placed on operationalizing the results, it is no longer democratic. This is a central point: for inquiry to be democratic, all those who have a say (Habermas would call these "stakeholders") must agree on the problem, the investigative route to be undertaken, what counts as results, and what counts as the solution. Anything less is undemocratic. In the contexts of schools, anything less is undemocratic education. If schools are to teach children democratic inquiry, they must ensure that inquiry is undertaken democratically and that their policies and procedures are not at odds with this goal.

This brings me to the matter at hand. Is Dewey consistent in the application of democratic inquiry in his own dealings with non-democratic nations? Does Dewey's model of democratic inquiry maintain its consistency throughout? Can, in other words, there be a way to understand Dewey's model of democratic inquiry that does not re-introduce authoritarianism, colonialism, and/or imperialism? I suggest that Dewey's writings on China from 1919–22 give us some hope that the answer is "yes."

MEANS AND ENDS IN CONTEXT:
DEWEY IN CHINA

China at the time of Dewey's visit was in the midst of the most far-reaching political transformation since the dawn of its empire over twenty centuries prior. The Q'ing Dynasty had been overthrown in 1911 and, rhetorically at least, the nation was a republic. Intellectuals from across the ideological spectrum debated the future of China, its academies and universities, and most of all, its politics. The years between 1911 and Dewey's visit were fertile ones but do not need to be discussed here. We can start with the situation Dewey faced when he arrived at Shanghai pot on 30 April 1919.

On 4 May 1919, a student- and intellectual-sponsored uprising began in Beijing and wound its way across the nation. It has been said that this May 4th movement attempted to displace Confucianism with individualism, borrowed largely from the west,[12] and that one of the schools of thought being advocated was Pragmatism. The central figure in bringing Pragmatism to China was Hu Shih, a student of Dewey's at Columbia University who had written his dissertation under Dewey in 1917 and completed the first volume of his *History of Chinese Philosophy* in 1919 – the year of the May 4th movement. Hu Shih was one of the vanguard of intellectuals who were calling for a repeal of the ancient Confucian tradition of rule-following, obedience to authority, and deference to elders in favour of democratic policies, practices, and (most important) thought.[13] At the same time, he was a leading figure in the quest to buttress support the vernacular literature of China.

At the time of the May 4th movement, China was a republic and owed its intellectual genesis (as well as its political influence) to Sun-Yat-Sen, the republican reformer who set out and became famous for the Three People's Principles, which held that China should be free, prosperous, and powerful.[14] However, feudal warlords, such as Yuan Shikai, eventually gained control of the provinces and, intellectually, little changed. After the Bolshevik Revolution of 1917, Sun curried favour with communist parties in the various provinces of China in order to boost his popularity and power. Students and intellectuals, however, were impatient with the lack of progress "on the ground," so to speak, and demanded immediate democratic reform, particularly of the universities. During the same period, Japan had established manufacturing facilities in Northern China (Manchuria) and in Shandong Province[15] and money were leaving China for Japan, while corrupt government officials looked the other way. Japan was thus the most recent occupying force in China, a pattern that had begun with Great Britain in the early nineteenth century.

The uprising began at Beida (Beijing University) in Beijing. At the time, Beida was run by Cai Yuanpei, a reformist administrator who had examined both German and French university systems and began to implement changes along the same lines.[16] Cai has been described as an anarchist who wanted to provide intellectual freedom for the faculty. He was ambivalent about the May 4th uprising and the American-style progressive education that was about to capture the intelligentsia in China.[17] However Cai admired Dewey and generally looked favourably on the transformation of the universities. In concert with Cai and other reformers at the time, progressive educators attempted to improve the plight of the least fortunate, particularly farmers, who constituted over eighty percent of the population.[18]

America's involvement in China was not ideologically consistent. On the one hand, the White House administration supported an "Open Door" policy with China, which included tariff relief and trade favouritism. With regard to education, it included the establishment of missions (most often Christian), such as the YMCA, which attempted to proselytize in favour of Christian morals and attitudes. The White House administration was, however, duplicitous: President Wilson supported the occupation of Shandong province by the Japanese.[19] Dewey, who was very unhappy with Wilson's about-face on China, and others thought that China could, with voluntary intervention on the part of the West (especially America), reform itself into a democracy. Dewey let Wilson and the American public know of his dissatisfaction in several articles written in 1921. The problem as Dewey saw it was the possibility that imperialism would be reintroduced into the nascent republic. He felt that America, by supporting European and Japanese interests, was risking just such a regression.[20]

The situation with respect to children in China was, by contemporary standards, dire. Most school-age children lived in rural areas and were expected to farm on coming of age. Formal education was sporadic; the Q'ing dynasty (and later, the Republic) had made schools available to the public, but most farmers were content to educate their children at home, with the result that literacy rates were extremely low.[21] Education in China was a luxury afforded to urban elites and those that surrounded them. The provincial schools that existed provided only the most rudimentary education and education was not seen as important in the largely rural peasant farmlands and villages across the nation. The vast majority of Chinese children received little education and what education they did receive was hardly recognizable as public in the common understanding of that term. This was a central concern of the student movements at the time.

It was during the first Republic that China adopted the famous "6-3-3" program. In 1922, children were granted six years of elementary school, three years of secondary school (for those that successfully passed their exams), and three to five years of advanced training, including university studies. The program had its roots in educational reforms that involved Dewey's progressivist followers, such as Hu Shih and Dao Xingzhi.[22] Normal schools were created for the instruction of teacher candidates. The curriculum itself changed: the emphasis

on Confucian ideals and the traditions of the ancient past gave
way to schooling in the areas of mathematics, natural sciences,
social sciences, fine arts, language, literature, and physical
culture. Teachers became increasingly militant, as unions
quickly sprang up. Not surprisingly, however, colleges and universities remained the provenance of the large cities: few universities were founded in the provinces and those that were,
were often hundreds of kilometres apart.

In contrast to the stratifications common to western nations,
the central social stratification in China was urban vs rural.[23]
Children in rural areas in the 1920s were *ceteris paribus* less
likely to benefit from a public education and far less likely to
attend college or university. The distance that divided peasant
from urban dweller and city from farm was the central barrier
preventing children from benefiting from public educational
institutions.[24] Most children subsisted on food drawn from the
land their families tended. In contrast to the large, and especially coastal, cities, where most of the intelligentsia resided,
education in the rural areas was largely accomplished through
family and community/village instruction. While life for these
children was no doubt difficult, and food was seldom in abun-
dance, their sense of identity was firmly entrenched in the
farming and village ethos.

Progressivists generally pushed to make schools public in
order to encourage literacy,[25] one of their chief goals, though
some have cast aspersions on the means used to achieve it.[26]
Some Progressivists allied themselves with the May 4th movement; others shied away from doing so. Dewey, however, supported the May 4th movement and was certainly implicated in
the rise of Progressivism in China. However, though he was
interested in improving the literacy of the Chinese, he focused
more on the larger social and political changes that were taking
place there and abroad. Hu Shih, one of Dewey's students
at Columbia, was a central figure in May 4th movement and
democratic principles had been proclaimed to replace ancient

laws, Dewey saw in China the possibility of a democratic transformation of society.[27] Central to this transformation was embracing science and the scientific method.[28]

Dewey had spent several months in Japan prior to his trip to China and witnessed what he saw as the backward, authoritarian nature of Japanese leadership. He was not taken with the Japanese educational system, nor with the political scene. Dewey's experience of China was very different. Almost immediately on arrival he sensed hopefulness, a willingness to change the course of intellectual society. Remarking on his journey from Japan to China, Dewey said, "It is doubtful whether anywhere in the world another journey of the same length brings with it such a complete change of political temper and belief ... Liberalism is in the air, but genuine liberals are encompassed with all sorts of difficulties especially in combining their liberalism with the devotion to theocratic roles which the imperialistic militarists who rule Japan have so skilfully thrown about the Throne and the Government."[29] Dewey then spent twenty-two months in Shanghai and Beijing, and traveled and toured the many provinces. He lectured voluminously: one estimate has him giving well over one hundred addresses.[30] Most importantly for my thesis, he wrote articles and briefs for American readers that were published in *The Dial* and *The New Republic*. It is these articles and briefs I wish to examine closely. Doing so reveals how little Dewey thought of the practice and possibility of "importing" democracy.

Early articles to *The New Republic* and *The Dial* focused on recent events in China, most notably the growing occupation by Japan. Dewey spoke of his admiration for the May 4th movement and the liberal sympathies he felt were regnant in China. Dewey also juxtaposed the situation in China with that in the United States. Drawing on his (early) experiences with the Chinese Zeitgeist, Dewey cast his eye to the West.

To go on opposing ideals and force to each other is to perpetuate this [Japanese] regime. The issue is not that of
indulging in ideals versus using force in a realistic way. As
long as we make this opposition we render our ideals impo-
tent, and we play into the hands of those who conceive
force as primarily military. Our idealism will never prosper
until it rests upon the organization and resolute use of the
greater forces of modern life: industry, commerce, finance,
scientific inquiry and discussion and the actualities of
human companionship.[31]

Indeed, Dewey never forgot the connection between events
abroad and the lessons they might provide for the United States,
liberalism, and democracy in general.

Much of his concern lay in the uses of science and scientific
inquiry. Though Dewey applauded the use of science in social
and political affairs, he did not think a seamless transition of
western methods to eastern societies was likely. In fact, he saw
in Japan the results of a too-facile acceptance of science and the
wedding of technological development to autocracy. "[T]he
standing minor premise of the conclusion of the recovery of
China by China is the protectorate of weak, unorganized and
unprogressive China by organized, militarized Japan – Japan
which has adopted western methods in science, industry, education and arms in order to turn them against the West and to pre-
serve the culture and territory of the East, of Asia, intact."[32]
China, to its credit, looked towards the United States for political guidance. Far from granting the United States the moral
high ground, however, Dewey felt that these responsibilities
demanded much more than might have seemed to be the case.
"Our country will have a hard time living up to the role for
which she has been cast. The difficulties are intellectual and
moral as well as matters of practical judgment and tact in
action. Have we the required fibre and virility? Or shall we once

more fall between a clever commercialism on the one hand and
a futile phrase-making idealism on the other? Above all, it
demands stamina and endurance of intelligence to think out a
consistent and workable plan and adhere to it."[33]

I believe the best way to understand Dewey's interpretation of
the relationship of the West (meaning for Dewey's purposes, the
United States) to China is through a dialectical frame. That is to
say, the question of the role that Western nations and Western
politics and economics were to play in fostering new growth of
China was intimately bound up with the possibility of China
developing *its own understanding and use* of these practices.

> The notion that, by the mere introduction of Western
> economy, China can be "saved," while it retains the old
> morality, the old set of ideas, the old Confucianism – or
> what genuine Confucianism had been petrified into – and
> the old family system, is the most utopian of sentimental
> idealisms. Economic and financial reform, unless it is
> accompanied by the growth of new ideals of culture, ethics
> and family life ... will merely shift the sore spots. It will
> remedy some evils and create others. Taken by itself it is a
> valuable practical measure. But it is the height of absurdity
> to use it as a stick with which to beat the aspirations of men
> and women, old as well as young, for new beliefs, new
> ideas, new methods of thought, new social and natural
> science – in short, for a New and Young China.[34]

The point is not that Confucianism is to be replaced by Western
political and economic models, though it must give way in some
respects; rather, whatever is done with these models must be
done in such a way that the process and the product are organic.
Changes to the economy of China can only effectively occur if
they are in harmony with correspondent changes in intellectual,
social, and cultural ideals. This is not a recommendation to

engage in sweeping ideological changes. *Prima facie*, this would be undemocratic. It is a recommendation to align economic changes with changes in other systems and institutions. Indeed, there can be no illusions that this will not involve upheaval. There can be no illusions that this will not be difficult, even painful, as scientific inquiry and its associated technologies transform the intellectual, social, and cultural landscape. "It is difficult to be patient with the notion that the industrial revolution can come in China without exercising far-reaching political, moral, domestic, and intellectual changes as it has wrought in Europe. Europe had its eighteenth century of change, involving destruction, even of good things, as well as introduction of new, good things."[35]

However, one would be mistaken to suggest that Dewey thought China's traditions were ripe for undermining change. Dewey does not think that these traditions will "go quietly." Nor does he think that they should. In a passage that should dispel any notions that Dewey insisted on outside interference in China's political and economic affairs, Dewey, commenting on the need for China to take responsibility for its own transformation, says,

We need to bear in mind that China will not be saved from outside herself ... China is used to taking time for her problems: she can neither understand nor profit by the impatient methods of the western world which are profoundly alien to her genius. Moreover, a civilization which is on a continental scale, which is so old that the rest of us are parvenus in comparison, which is thick and closely woven, cannot be hurried in its development without disaster. Transformation from within is its sole way out, and we can best help China by trying to see to it that she gets the time she needs in order to effect this transformation, whether or not we like the particular form it assumes at any particular time.[36]

Dewey also provides specific examples of how these inquiries have already transformed this landscape. For example, "the modern methods born of the industrial revolution, which fatuous observers would introduce while they dream of leaving old institutions unchanged. The railway and the factory system are undermining the family system. They will continue to do so, even if every student takes the vow of eternal silence."[37] Nevertheless, Dewey has to provide an argument as to how this change is to take place democratically. He believes that opposition to current programs, which in the case of China means the authoritarian nature of the empire, is, and must be, developed.

As is always the case, official opposition stimulates the movement of ideas. The menace of autocracy from within and without gives edge and fire to the hunger for new ideas. The eagerness grows for knowledge of the thought of liberal western countries in just the degree in which the powers near at hand in Tokyo and Peking seem to symbolize an intellectual creed which the world has outgrown. The more the so-called political revolution exhibits itself as a failure, the more active is the demand for an intellectual revolution which will make some future political revolution a reality.[38]

Note that it is the *intellectual* opposition of those under the authoritarian regime that will initiate the change and not outside forces. Once change is underway, a more programmatic response to the issues and concerns of the public can begin. "For Young China also passed through a state of optimism and belief in wholesale change; a subsequent state of disillusionment and pessimism; and, in a third stage, has now settled down to constructive efforts along the lines of education, industry, and social reorganization."[39] This intellectual revolution partly "comes in consequence of the growth of science, industry and commerce, and of the new human relations and responsibilities they produce; ... it springs from education, from the enlightenment of the people, and from special training in the knowledge and technical skill required in the administration of the modern state."[40]

The claim that China's intellectual community can develop these programs turns on the possibility that this community can make decisions independent of foreign intervention. Indeed, it *insists* on this. Dewey thought he saw in the May 4th movement signs of this independence, of this wanting to work out the understandings and uses of the scientific method and the technology it introduces. "They [Young China] are profoundly resentful of all efforts which condescendingly hold up Western institutions, political, religious, educational, as models to be humbly accepted and submissively repeated. They are acutely aware that the spirit of imitation at the expense of initiative and independence of thought has been the chief cause of China's retrogression, and they do not propose to shift the model; they intend to transform the spirit."[41] This would presumably include religious institutions in China, as well as religious practices, though the caveat regarding Dewey's understanding of the full-scale implications of such reform remains.

Dewey believed that the May 4th movement understood the far-reaching implications of this transformation.

There is nothing which one hears so often from the lips of the representatives of Young China of today as that education is the sole means of reconstructing China … There is an enormous interest in making over the traditional family system, in overthrowing militarism, in extension of local self-government, but always the discussion comes back to education, to teachers and students, as the central agency in promoting other reforms."[42]

The Young China movement was sceptical of tradition, including religious thought and practice. In place of Daoism, Confucianism, and Buddhism, Young China advocated a secular program of science and technology. Dewey's predication that the old empire, together with its attendant cultural and intellectual practices, would fall seemed inevitable when he looked at the situation through the eyes of his former students, especially Hu Shih.

This brings me to the question of the role of other nations in the development of scientific inquiry and the associated technologies this inquiry produces. I have shown that scientific inquiry is for Dewey the means to democratic living. Scientific inquiry is what helps us (as a public) move towards breaking down those barriers of communication that inhibit us from understanding one another and, more urgently, help us ameliorate social problems. Scientific inquiry is not coeval with the science done in laboratory environments or research labs, though it includes it. Dewey hoped and thought that it was possible for all citizens to have a sufficient grasp of scientific inquiry to understand the importance of shared problem finding and solving, and to work through experimentation to arrive at a solution that works. Indeed, he believed that it is only through the solution to community problems that one's individual growth is augmented. The capacity of social institutions to modify themselves so that inquiry is amenable to the public (a sort of "publicity condition" in John Rawls's sense of the term) is the formal arrangement of inquiry that Dewey connotes as democracy.

If this is correct, if the very idea of democracy rests on the possibility of a public finding and solving its own problems or the problems of certain of its members and then experimenting towards a satisfactory solution, then there can be no question of foreign "interference" in these matters. It cannot be the case that Western nations can implant democracy, scientific inquiry, or associated technologies. These must be chosen and assistance from those knowledgeable in their theory and application requested. Such a stance leads Dewey to conclude that any foreign involvement is to be premised on "a definite and open policy, openly arrived at by discussion at home and made known to all the world. Then we need to be prepared to back it up with action."[43] Nor can there be any question of Western nations themselves remaining isolationist or undemocratic. "The dilemma is that while our day of isolation is over, international affairs are still conducted upon a basis and by methods that were instituted before democracy was heard of as a political fact. Hence we engage in foreign policies only at the risk of harming even such imperfect internal democracy as we have already achieved."[44]

The art of international negotiation and compromise, of assistance over and above colonizing, was poorly developed in the early part of the twentieth century. Dewey certainly recognized this. "Diplomacy is still the home of the exclusiveness, the privacy, and the unchecked love of power and prestige, and one may say the stupidity, characteristic of every oligarchy. Democracy has not touched it. Beware of contamination through contact. That, I think, is the sound instinct behind our aversion to foreign entanglement."[45] Until diplomatic methods improved, there could be no mitigation of the fear of outside involvement in national affairs. Nevertheless, such outside involvement was necessary, indeed crucial, to China's appropriation of technology and could not be neglected. The question of concern in contemporary international relations is whether these methods have improved. I shall have more to say about this further. For now, I wish only to note one area in which Dewey *did* discuss specific responsibilities of involvement and this is, not surprisingly, in education. "China does not need copies of American colleges, but it does still need colleges supported by foreign funds and in part manned by well trained foreigners who are capable of understanding Chinese needs, alert, agile, sympathetic in their efforts to meet them."[46] What America can do is help by "freeing those men [sic] who are adapting their curriculum and methods to Chinese conditions against the petty opposition and nagging they now meet from reactionaries."[47] This last sentence deserves commentary. What does it mean to "free those men?" On one reading, this seems to suggest interference in the public's capacity to inquire. Does it mean to emancipate them politically? Economically? Intellectually? I claim that the only legitimate interpretation of this passage requires taking into account the context of Dewey's concerns regarding democracy. If we focus on the need for public problem finding and solving, experimenting, and evaluating differing possibilities until a solution is found, then we can only conclude that intervention should be welcomed (by those members of the public that have the problem) and limited to guidance, but *not* involved in the decision-making itself. *A problem can only be genuine if it is undertaken and solved by those that have the problem: other 'solutions' are chimerical.*

DEMOCRACY, CULTURE, AND EDUCATION

There are lessons for today in Dewey's understanding of the May 4th movement in China. First, democracy is not a commodity subject to importation, the way we often think of technologies, goods, and certain services. Technologies, tools, even ideas, can be brought into a nation and taken up by its experts or its public. Democracy, however, cannot. On Dewey's reading of democracy, it is the possibility of the public inquiring into and solving shared problems through the formalized means of social institutions that makes for a democracy, not procedures, goods and services, or technologies per se. As Dewey saw it, the May 4th movement was attempting to persuade the public of China to become democratic, as opposed to having the republic "adopt" democracy. Persuaded by pamphlets, protests, rallies, and assemblies, the May 4th movement was behaving democratically in order to convince the public that democratic means and ends are the best way to solve problems. Despite this, the May 4th movement, and particularly Hu Shih, have been criticized for neglecting and/or abandoning China's cultural heritage for the sake of Western, scientific ideals.[48] Hu often cloaked democracy in the rhetoric of worship and played on the proclivities of the Chinese for deference in their beliefs about science and scientific method. The common nicknames for Dewey – "Mr. Democracy," and "Mr. Science" – terms coined by the dean of liberal arts at Beida University, Chen Duxiu, testify to the tendency to make Dewey a spokesperson for a monolithic, even authoritarian, concept of democratic living.[49] Indeed, as Wang maintains, though Dewey's lectures were not mistranslated, "Nonetheless, we may reasonably believe that Hu may have occasionally altered the meanings of what Dewey said to highlight a particular point to promote a certain agenda. Even though these occasional anomalies may seem minor, they eventually affected the way Chinese intellectuals responded to Dewey."[50]

This was not the only embellishment of Dewey's lectures. Beyond the possible mistranslation of Dewey's lectures, of which literally thousands of copies were circulated, a larger mistranslation, or perhaps, intentional misinterpretation, took place. It is Wang's contention that,

> Dewey came to China at the perfect time for his own learning. His teaching, however, was compromised by the intellectual climate during the May Fourth era. Owing to the ideological divisiveness of the time, Chinese intellectuals tended to use Dewey to serve their own agendas rather than engage his ideas directly. They either hailed him as a savior or denigrated him as a false god. In fact, one senses that Dewey's status as teacher was symbolic at best. His teachings were largely mediated through the interpretations of Hu Shih, who differed from Dewey in many important ways. Hu advocated wholesale assimilation to Western values and beliefs, whereas Dewey hoped that China would maintain the strengths in her own culture as a basis for future development.[51]

And while we may not wish to completely accept Wang's understanding of Dewey's reception in China, we should acknowledge that there may well have been ideological and interpretive differences between Dewey and his Chinese supporters.

The May 4th movement was influenced by Western ideals. The central figures in the movement, including Hu Shih, were educated in the West and brought the ideals of a democratic public back to China. These ideals were in the main inimical to traditional Chinese familial structures and dismissive of Daoist, Confucian, Buddhist, and other religious/philosophical influences. The great irony here, in contradistinction to the findings of other chapters in this book, is that Chinese religion, by which I mean the Confucian and Daoist traditions, *played very little if any role in the uptake of Dewey`s thought by leading Chinese scholars*. Indeed, it is not too much of a stretch to say that these thinkers were *more secular* (in the Western senses of the term) than Dewey on the issue of reconstituting China through abandonment of its heritage. The Confucian ideals of rule-following, principle (*Li*), and obedience to authority, seemingly ingrained in Chinese social practices, were not part of the goals of Dewey's interpreters, such as Hu Shih. The personifications of science and democracy, and the law-like understandings that arose as a result of the uptake of these Western notions further complicate this state of affairs. The mass dissemination of terms such as "democracy" was evidently given a Confucian turn by various media outlets, so that democracy (and science) was rendered in ambiguous ways that did not concur with the way they were understood in the West.[52] The configurations of democracy developed in these various interpretations were so convoluted that it is a wonder the intelligent lay public of China could make any sense of what was at stake.

Nevertheless, we would be mistaken to conclude that the *Western ideals themselves* constituted democracy and that these were what the May 4th members attempted to put into practice. The ideals themselves were just that: ideals. *Democratic publics are imagined in ideals, but democratic publics are not realized in them. What Dewey foresaw was the merging of a (Western) ideal with existing (Chinese) ideals, not the importation of democratic, Western practices to China.*[53] This view seems to contradict the goals of certain May 4th reformers. The difference between Dewey and certain of his interpreters is revealing: for Dewey, it is the public itself that must decide whether to develop and follow democratic practices, not the intellectuals and certainly not Western nations. To act otherwise would be to violate the requirement that democratic ends be aligned with democratic means: in this case, the "end" of a public, democratic process with the instantiation of Western, democratic practices.

This brings me to the question of the role of "experts" for the public. It seems that here we can criticize the May 4th movement (and by implication, Dewey) as have been too wedded to the idea of an expert class and, indeed, functioning as an expert class themselves.[54] I have dealt with this as a problem intrinsic to Dewey's progressivism in other contexts.[55] Here, I wish to re-iterate a point I have said in these other works. The role of experts in a democracy is limited to suggestion and guidance, *not* policy-making. This would apply to Chinese intellectuals as well as to other nations who are acting in the role of experts, supplying ideas and technologies (as well as goods and services). Dewey makes this quite clear in *The Public and Its Problems*. As Dewey says, "It is not necessary that the many should have the knowledge and skill to carry on the needed [scientific and social] investigations; what is required is that they have the ability to judge of the bearing of the knowledge supplied by others upon common concerns."[56] Other nations may reasonably demand that the goods, services, and intellectual tools provided be used in a way that is congruent with their practices. For example, certain technologies may not be used for military purposes, or certain educational models may not be used to subvert public will. These agreements are often bargained for in good faith, but there may be clauses in formal agreements that spell out the conditions in which a service or technology ceases. In fact, there is good reason to suppose that the adoption of Western technologies and certain (scientific) ideas and ideals did occur, *without* the corresponding democratic ideals that had allowed this science, in other contexts, to flourish. This situation has not changed of late.[57] What makes a democracy is not the importation of goods, services, technologies, or even ideals, though at some level this seems unavoidable. Again, it is the capacity of a public to carry out a form of living (Dewey calls this "associated living") that fosters the finding and solving of human problems.

LAST THOUGHTS

By way of a discussion of Dewey's experience of the student movement in China, I have dwelt on the perils of importing and exporting democracy. My thesis is that there can be no possibility of democratic education unless a public has a genuine need or interest in developing such an education. This requires, at a minimum, that the public begin the quest for problem finding and solving necessary to undertake and complete this task. It also militates against experts or bureaucrats managing the process without direction and oversight from the public. It certainly excludes the direct importation of any purportedly democratic educational system. Such decisions must be made by the public, for the public, a process that seems to negate the possibility that there can be a facile transplantation of institutions and practices. I maintain that, if education is to be truly democratic, it must be "home-grown." Any purported democratic education foisted on a public is, *ex hypothesi*, undemocratic.

The failure of the May 4th movement to galvanize the learned public in China is attributable to many things, not the least of which was the misrepresentation of Dewey's lectures and writings to an ambivalent, though open to change, audience. Translators of Dewey, particularly, Hu Shih, told audiences and politicians what he thought they should hear and not necessarily what Dewey believed about political or social matters. If his interlocutors had been better able to understand Dewey, they might have heard him say that only China can develop China in a democratic direction: that only the public can render systematic changes to social policies and practices, and that only the will of the people can foster the sort of democratic spirit of inquiry and imagination that is required for a legitimate democracy to take root. Unfortunately, the Chinese public and politicians did not hear this, or, rather, heard it in the context of either radical overhaul of China's political and social legacies (Hu Shih) or as the call for authoritarian obedience to a new political arrangement. Neither of these would have been acceptable to Dewey, who maintained at great lengths that it is not imposition, but inquiry, that results in democratic living.

Dewey's articles in *The New Republic* and *The Dial* remind us that democracy is a practice conducted by the public of a nation and not a commodity for trade or exchange. Nevertheless, much of what counts as trade or exchange is done under the auspices of "democracy" or "democratic practice," in one sense or another, and this misleading characterization insinuates itself into educational discussions as well. Well-known examples of this abound. First, there is the conflation of language training with democracy. Here, the argument is that democratic citizens will be more likely to be formed if multilingual societies are created. Admittedly, there is some truth to this: multilingual citizens will have a broader and deeper grasp of diverse cultural and linguistic contexts that may result in a more readily sympathetic understanding of others. However, what results is *not* democracy. It may lead to a cosmopolitical sentiment, but it does not help the public of a nation confront its own problems with an eye to a solution – at least, not directly.

Dewey's recognition of a public as that body of individuals making decisions in concert is frustrated by authoritarian practices. This is particularly the case with respect to school-age children. Authoritarian practices consist of practices that the public has not agreed to, while institutional educational practices that are put into place against or without the consent of the public create and promote a barrier between the public and its ability to meet the needs and desires of its children. By itself this may or may not herald the disenfranchisement of children; the likelihood, however, is that it will. Issues of public concern will largely go unattended and/or unaddressed in situations where practices are implemented in a top-down manner. This leaves the public (and *a fortiori*, the children) with little opportunity to enact change if when faced with these practices. The point here is not that authoritarian intervention will marginalize children, though that may indeed occur. Rather, it is that the public has no means of redress if marginalization occurs. Even if the public is able to locate and identify a problem common to groups of school-children, its ability to contain and/or transform the situation is negligible. This leaves the potential for democracy dubious.

The goal, then, has to be one of ensuring democratic polity and procedures while maintaining a public that is sufficiently cohesive to break down barriers that inhibit children's growth. This is obviously no easy task: it assumes that the public can (and will) organize successfully to solve the "problem." However successful a democracy is, there can be no guarantee that the public will band together with enough strength to carry this out. The problem is not so much the unwillingness to embrace democratic practices, though this is obviously a concern: rather, the problem is the need to develop a unity of purpose and law while maintaining democratic practice. We are reminded once again of Rousseau's paradox: a democracy *eo ipso* cannot force the public to speak with one voice. If the public speaks with one voice, the question of providing democratic means to ensure that the minority voices are heard amongst the majority voices comes to the fore. These minority voices cannot be simply marginalized. Nor, however, can they be followed, if following them leads to a fractured public. To follow the minority voices under these conditions is to admit that the public does not speak with one voice; yet this is precisely the condition needed if a democracy is to function in both theory and practice. If theories about democracy are unable to mount a sufficient response to this challenge, the alternative is, as Dewey might put it, to strive for continuity and consistency in practice through the insurance of democratic ends aligned with democratic means. The only acceptable democratic position is one in which the public has the means to make the choice of self-determination and this requires that democracy and democratic education not be conducted from without.

NOTES

1 For more on these examples, see the Introduction by Sor-hoon Tan and John Whalen-Bridge in *Democracy as Culture: Deweyan Pragmatism in a Globalizing World*, ed. Sor-hoon Tan and John Whalen-Bridge (Albany: SUNY Press, 2008).

2 I am by no means the first to suggest the instructive quality of Dewey's writings on China. For a full estimation of the bearing of Deweyan pragmatism on Confucian thought, see Sor-hoon Tan, *Confucian Democracy: A Deweyan Reconstruction* (Albany: SUNY Press, 2004).

3 John Dewey, "Democracy and Education," in *John Dewey: The Middle Works, 1899–1924*, vol. 9, 1916, ed. J. Boydston (Carbondale: Southern Illinois University Press, 1980), 93.

4 Ibid., 88–9. Italics mine.

5 Ibid., 91.

6 John Dewey, "Freedom and Culture," in *John Dewey: The Later Works, 1925–1952*, vol. 13, 1938–39, ed. J. Boydston (Carbondale: Southern Illinois University Press, 1987), 187.

7 See James Scott Johnston, *Inquiry in Education: John Dewey and the Quest for Democracy* (Albany: SUNY Press, 2006).

8 John Dewey, "Experience and Nature," in *John Dewey: The Later Works, 1925–1952*, vol. 1, 1925, ed. J. Boydston (Carbondale: Southern Illinois University Press, 1981), 210.

9 John Dewey, "Experience and Education," in *John Dewey:The Later Works, 1925–1952*, vol. 13, 1938–39, ed. J. Boydston (Carbondale: Southern Illinois University Press, 1987), 19.

10 John Dewey, "Experience and Nature," 308–9.

11 People are silenced in different ways. Some of this silencing, I would argue, is the unhappy consequence of pre-existing power relations made manifest in democratic discourses. Those already positioned to benefit from democratic discourse will likely do so, perhaps at the expense of others. Is this a good reason to constrain democratic discourse? If the answer is "yes," then democracy is not being practiced. If on the other hand, the answer is "no," legitimate power differences may continue to affect discourse. I cannot get into the difficulty here, but it seems to me that, given the quandary, Dewey would side with democratic practice.

12 This is now a controversial claim. Jie Qi, "A History of the Present: Chinese Intellectuals, Confucianism and Pragmatism," in *Inventing the Modern Self and John Dewey: Modernities and the Traveling of Pragmatism in Education*, ed. T. Popkewitz (New York: Palgrave MacMillan, 2006), 255–77 and Antonio S. Cua, "Emergence of the History of Chinese Philosophy," in *Comparative Approaches to Chinese Philosophy*, ed. Bo Mou (London: Ashgate, 2003), 3–32, as well as Ruth Hayhoe, "Cultural Tradition and Educational Modernization: Lessons from the Republican Era," in *Education and Modernization: The Chinese Experience*, ed. Ruth Hayhoe (Oxford: Pergammon Press, 1992), 47–72, argue that the May 4th Movement,

and particularly Hu Shih, tried to supplant Confucianism. This is true if we consider Confucianism as authoritarian. For more on the differences between Confucianism, Daoism, and Western thought, see Kwong-loi Shun, "On the Idea of Axiology in Pre-Modern Chinese," in *Chinese Philosophy in an Era of Globalization*, ed. Robin Wang (Albany: SUNY Press, 2004), 37–44. Others, however, suggest a more integrative strategy, melding what was good and right about Confucianism and Daoism with Western thought. The wholesale repudiation of the Confucian tradition is not the case if Confucianism is seen as a cultural manifestation of arts and literature. This is what we see in Hu Shih's attempt at developing the Chinese vernacular. See also D.W.Y. Kwok, *Scientism in Chinese Thought: 1900–1950* (New Haven: Yale University Press, 1965). Kwok sees Hu Shih as attempting to meld pragmatism with ancient Chinese thought. See in particular, his discussion of the early Q'ing scholars' empiricism (1644–1781).

13 Jessica Ching-Sze Wang, *John Dewey in China: To Teach and To Learn* (Albany: SUNY Press, 2007), 38, and Sor-hoon Tan, "Reconstructing 'Culture': A Deweyan Response to Antidemocratic Culturalism," in *Democracy as Culture: Deweyan Pragmatism in a Globalizing World* (Albany: SUNY Press, 2008), 31–53. Again, the verdict is out on how deep the repudiation of Confucian tradition goes.

14 Sun-Yat-Sen wrote these in 1905. It is important to note that Dewey was not the only Western intellectual embraced by the Chinese. Indeed, German idealism was perhaps more popular amongst the reformers than Deweyan pragmatism-at least until the May 4th movement. A number of reformers, for example, embraced the ethics of Immanuel Kant through the writings of Kant's biographer, Friedrich Paulsen. And we cannot forget those that embraced Marxist-Leninism, which Sun-Yat-Sen flirted with.

15 This was largely a result of the republic's acquiescence to the economic might of Japan. Monies flowed in, in exchange for land and workers, and resulted in a wealthy if pusillanimous government.

16 Ruth Hayhoe, *China's Universities 1895–1995: A Century of Cultural Conflict*, (New York: Garland Publishing, Inc, 1996).

17 For my purposes, progressive education is that education, beginning with Rousseau, that privileges the nature and experiences of the child over the inculcation of the curriculum. Deweyan progressivism was thus one among many progressivisms in education; it was most closely allied with the social-democratic interests of the reformers of society at the turn of the twentieth century.

18 Hayhoe, "Cultural Tradition and Educational Modernization"; Alexander Woodside, "Real and Imagined Continuities in the Chinese Struggle for Literacy," in *Education and Modernization: The Chinese Experience*, ed. Ruth Hayhoe (Oxford: Pergammon Press, 1992), 23–46.

19 Jerry Israel, *Progressivism and the Open Door: America and China, 1905–1921* (Pittsburgh: University of Pittsburgh Press, 1971), 121, 181.

20 John Dewey, "A Parting of the Ways for America," in *John Dewey: The Middle Works, 1899–1924*, vol. 13, 1921–22, ed. J. Boydston (Carbondale: Southern Illinois University Press, 1983), 170–1.

21 Alexander Woodside, "Real and Imagined Continuities in the Chinese Struggle for Literacy."

22 In 1919, Dewey attended the 5th conference of United Education Ministry in Taiyuan. Dewey's student Hu Shih also attended. The speeches Dewey gave while in Taiyuan were on school reform and the experimental attitude in education. Prof. Menglu, a student of Dewey at Columbia University, attended the 7th conference of the United Education Ministry in Guangzhou in 1921, which produced the penultimate draft of the 6-3-3 program. Menglu was a vociferous propagandist on behalf of progressive education generally and Deweyan progressive education in particular.

23 Woodside, "Real and Imagined Continuities in the Chinese Struggle for Literacy," 23–46.

24 This situation, while somewhat mitigated, continues today: there is currently a large influx of farming populations into the large cities (e.g., Shanghai) as the industrial and manufacturing economy of China booms. Those entering the cities soon find that the doors open

to the burgeoning middle and upper middle classes are closed to them.

25 Woodside, "Real and Imagined Continuities in the Chinese Struggle for Literacy."

26 Alexander Woodside claims that the peasants may not have thought literacy to be as important as the Progressivists did. This may also be the case with respect to public schooling: traditionally, Chinese education has been a private, often family, affair, with the exception of the gentry. Schools were offered, not imposed. Yet, as Woodside suggests, Progressivists wished to impose public schooling on the children, without (perhaps) taking into consideration the wants of the peasantry. If this were fact the case, it would seem to violate the democratic means/ends maxim necessitated by Deweyan thinking. However, the use of the experimental method (as Hu Shih wished) precludes this. See Woodside, "Real and Imagined Continuities in the Chinese Struggle for Literacy," esp. 42–3.

27 John Dewey, "On the Two Sides of the Eastern Sea," in *John Dewey: The Middle Works, 1899–1924*, vol. 11, 1918–19, ed. J. Boydston (Carbondale: Southern Illinois University Press, 1982), 174–9.

28 Hu Shih, in Kwok, *Scientism in Chinese Thought*, 92. This has led some critics of progressivism in China to make much of Dewey's so-called allegiance to all things scientific. However, as Wang points out, this is based on an embellishment of Dewey's scientific rhetoric by those, such as Hu, interested in wholesale change of political and economic practices. Indeed, Hu Shih would later proclaim that science must be worshipped.

29 John Dewey, "On the Two Sides of the Eastern Sea."

30 Qi, "A History of the Present."

31 John Dewey, "The Discrediting of Idealism," in *John Dewey: The Middle Works, 1899–1924*, vol. 11, 1918–19, ed. J. Boydston (Carbondale: Southern Illinois University Press, 1982), 185.

32 John Dewey, "The International Duel in China," in *John Dewey: The Middle Works, 1899–1924*, vol. 11, 1918–19, ed. J. Boydston (Carbondale: Southern Illinois University Press, 1982), 193.

33 Ibid., 197.

34 John Dewey, "Old China and New," in *John Dewey: The Middle Works, 1899–1924*, vol. 13, 1921–22, ed. J. Boydston (Carbondale: Southern Illinois University Press, 1983), 103.

35 Ibid., 105.

36 John Dewey, "A Parting of the Ways for America,"170–1.

37 John Dewey, "Old China and New," 104.

38 John Dewey, "Our National Dilemma," in *John Dewey: The Middle Works, 1899–1924*, vol. 12, 1920, ed. J. Boydston (Carbondale: Southern Illinois University Press, 1982), 4.

39 John Dewey, "The New Leaven in Chinese Politics," in *John Dewey: The Middle Works, 1899–1924*, vol. 12, 1920, ed. J. Boydston (Carbondale: Southern Illinois University Press, 1982), 49.

40 Ibid.

41 John Dewey, "America and Chinese Education," in *John Dewey: The Middle Works, 1899–1924*, vol. 13, 1921–22, ed. J. Boydston (Carbondale: Southern Illinois University Press, 1983), 230.

42 Ibid.

43 John Dewey, "The International Duel in China," 198.

44 John Dewey, "Our National Dilemma," 5.

45 Ibid., 7.

46 John Dewey, "America and Chinese Education," 232.

47 Ibid., 231.

48 Ruth Hayhoe, in "Cultural Tradition and Educational Modernization," makes this claim on the basis of her research into the debates surrounding the progressive school system.

49 Though the terms were in circulation several years before Dewey arrived in Shanghai, his presence quickly led to the attribution of these personifications to him. Dewey's students did not discourage this.

50 Wang, *John Dewey in China*, 31. Wang surmises this on the basis of an interpretation of one of Dewey's lectures by Hu Shih. Hu is reported to have translated Dewey as saying there is no social or gender hierarchy in America, which of course it is very doubtful that

Dewey would have maintained. The quote is from Dewey's lecture, *Democratic Developments in America*.

51 Ibid., 83.

52 For example, see Guantao Gin and Qingfeng Liu, "From 'Republicanism' to 'Democracy': China's Selective Adoption and Reconstruction of Modern Western Political Concepts 1840–1924," *History of Political Thought* 26, no. 3 (Autumn, 2005): 467–501.

53 Wang concurs. She says, "Dewey understood that democracy for China has to come from her own cultural roots rather than from the imposition by foreign influences." Unfortunately, Wang continues, "Chinese intellectuals, including his own disciple Hu, failed to take his advice. In the end, the biggest beneficiary of this intercultural exchange was perhaps Dewey himself." Wang, *John Dewey in China*, 83.

54 See again, Hayhoe, "Cultural Tradition and Educational Modernization."

55 See the claims I make in James Scott Johnston, *Inquiry and Education: John Dewey and the Quest for Democracy* (New York: SUNY Press, 2006), esp. 126–31.

56 John Dewey, "The Public and Its Problems," in *John Dewey: The Later Works, 1925–1952*, vol. 2, 1925–27, ed. J. Boydston (Carbondale: Southern Illinois University Press, 1984), 367.

57 Recently, a neo-conservative turn has taken place amongst Chinese intellectuals; these intellectuals are wary of progressivist approaches to the public and are particularly sceptical of what they see as the pragmatic acquiescence to tradition in progressivist thinkers such as Hu Shih. According to Joseph Fewsmith, this is part of a larger critique of the "Enlightenment tradition" that began in the late 1990s and continued (at least) into the early 2000s. Some of this is political: the perceived alliance of the May 4th movement with Western and, particularly, American interests, is one reason. The other was a reaction to an upsurge in interest in the Enlightenment among intellectuals in China, particularly in the 1980s. Of course, Hu Shih has been pilloried before, most

famously during the 1950s when academics were forced to recant their earlier progressivism and declare communism triumphant. See Joseph Fewsmith, *China since Tiananmen: The Politics of Transition* (Cambridge: Cambridge University Press, 2001), 183.

3

Readings of the Pedagogy of John Dewey in Spain in the Early Twentieth Century
Reconciling Pragmatism and Transcendence

GONZALO JOVER

INTRODUCTION

The turn of the nineteenth to the twentieth century in Spain was characterized by a deep feeling of crisis that led to an attempt at national regeneration in which education was given a key role. At the end of the nineteenth century, many Spanish children were tremendously underprivileged: they were still a widespread source of cheap labour and attempts at providing elementary education to the general public had as yet met with little success.[1] To alleviate this situation, legislative and institutional measures were taken (such as the Ministry of Public Instruction and Fine Arts, created in 1900), based on important new ideas that had come in with the new century, although they had not always achieved the desired ends. Further change was sought by introducing innovations that were being carried out in other countries. In consequence, in the first three decades of the twentieth century an extraordinary amount of activity took place in receiving the ideas and writings of authors involved in the new education movement, particularly Édouarde Claparède, Adolphe Ferrière, Ovide Decroly, Maria Montessori, George Kerschensteiner, and John Dewey. Several reasons explain this newfound interest. The most important, as noted by M. Mar del Pozo, was that "as a result of the desperation pervading Spanish society in 1898, the word 'new' acquired a special meaning as a symbol of the much-needed change to overcome the existing situation, unwanted and depressing, and move towards a brighter future, in which our nation would regain its former splendour."[2]

Spain's 1898 defeat in the war with the United States had been a turning point in the Spanish people's self-perception, leading to a generalized feeling that they had forever lost the place they had held in history for centuries. While they may all have shared this feeling, there was little agreement on how the causes of the situation should be understood and what should be done to correct it. For conservatives, the loss of traditional values had caused the pervasive sense of decline and they therefore advocated continuing the traditions represented by the Catholic Church and the monarchy. To progressive liberals, however, the situation was proof of the nation's backwardness, and they pushed for radical modernization. For them, Dewey and pragmatism signified an attitude of openness to the future, "a philosophy which regards the world as being in continuous formation, where there is still place for indeterminism, for the new and for a real future."[3] This vision of a world left to its own devices was not, of course, acceptable within traditional Spanish pedagogy, which was firmly rooted in the Catholic Church.[4] Dewey's name thus remained associated with movements that attempted to modernize the nation by renovating education.

The purpose of this chapter is to re-examine the understanding that one of these movements – the Free Teaching Institute (Institución Libre de Enseñanza) – had of Dewey in the early twentieth century. Current studies on the presence of Dewey's ideas in turn-of-the-century educational reforms have shown that the pedagogic and political elements of his system were read in different ways, ways that suggest the need for more local approaches and oblige us to shift our focus in research from the process of influence to the process of reception.[5] The concept of "reading" emphasizes this change in approach. We must shift our attention from the point of origin of these ideas in Dewey's works and, while not completely losing sight of what was actually said, focus on the process of adoption; on the way his ideas were re-worked during the process of integration into a different framework than the one they had been created to address.

HISTORICAL BACKGROUND

The Free Teaching Institute was founded by Francisco Giner de los Ríos in 1876 as an autonomous institution free from state and church control. It epitomized the values of progressive liberalism in both the political and ethical sense, and was linked to varying degrees with many of the pedagogical experiments involved in attempts to modernize the turn-of-the-century educational system, such as the Museo Pedagógico Nacional (National Pedagogical Museum), headed by Manuel Bartolomé Cossio, the Cátedra de Pedagogía Superior (University Chair in Higher Pedagogy), the Junta para Ampliación de Estudios e Investigaciones Científicas (Council for the Extension of Scientific Study and Research), the Escuela Superior del Magisterio (Higher School of Teaching, in which some of its members participated), the Instituto-Escuela (Institute-School), the school colonies associated with the hygienist movement, etc.[6]

Originally, the Institute's educational project was based on the philosophy of Karl Christian Friedrich Krause and the pedagogy of Friedrich Froebel, who were united in the idea that education should focus on the human being as human being.[7] Giner de los Rios referred to this ideal by pointing out that "what Spain needs and must ask of the school is not people that can read and write: what Spain needs are 'complete human beings,' and training them requires educating the body as much as the spirit, and willingness as much as if not more than understanding."[8]

Krause's philosophy was introduced in Spain in the mid-1800s by Julián Sanz del Rio, and variations made to it by successive generations had turned it, as the Catalonian philosopher and pedagogue Joaquin Xirau said, into an open moral discipline sustained by freedom of research and conscience, among whose ranks "can be found Hegelians, Kantian, positivists, ... Catholics, free-thinkers ... It detests only the opaque and stiff skeleton of decadent scholastics."[9] Sanz del Río's decision to introduce Krausism had not been capricious, nor was it a sign of intellectual dullness, as the most conservative sectors, who saw it as a threat to traditional values, maintained. There were several conditions that encouraged its acceptance. Among these were the humanistic, mystical, and even openly religious elements present in Krause's harmonic rationalism, which were more in accord with Spanish beliefs than many other philosophies.[10] As Solomon Lipp summarized, "Spanish intellectuals, while rebelling against what they considered to be theological dogmatism, nevertheless experienced a need to fill a spiritual vacuum. Krausism seemed to be the answer: it represented reason, moral rectitude, and freedom, as opposed to what these intellectuals viewed as corruption, hypocrisy, and absolutism."[11] In Krause's harmonic rationalism, they saw the way to a free and sincere religiousness that was compatible with Catholicism and was open, in intimate contact with God through the world, while also providing a strong sense that the goal of humanity was to achieve the ideal of the harmony of fellowship for every man and woman with other human beings, with nature, and with God.

In March 1870, Karl Röder, jurist and disciple of Krause, sent a letter to Giner de los Ríos in which he highlighted the affinities between the German and Spanish peoples in dealing with upcoming changes. Röder especially emphasized the regionalist and ethnic spirit and the "strong sense of human dignity, energy, and true religiousness" of the Spanish people as opposed to the centralism and "the multitude of false doctrines imported from France."[12] To look at the situation in this way however, is to over-simplify the religious tone of Spanish society of the time and underestimate the importance of religion to Spanish Krausists. In answer to a letter in which the Krausist Hermann Karl von Leonhardi asked about the Old Catholics and the religious stance of Sanz del Río's followers,[13] Giner de los Ríos draws a much more complex picture of the situation in Spain. He identifies a small number of Old Catholics who had little influence and were more concerned with politics than with religious life; an increasing group of ultramontane Catholics faithful to Rome; a minority of advocates of the reformed church; some professionals and many workers who, following the International, were openly atheist; and a large number of enlightened youth who were uninterested in any religious vision and disdainful of any form of positive religion. In addition to those groups, Giner de los Ríos continues, most of the population, regardless of religious practices, were indifferent to religion and concerned themselves exclusively with their own affairs. Not even the Spanish Krausists had a uniform stance toward religion. Giner de los Ríos disdainfully hints at a statement made by "some of our dissidents" who had become more sympathetic to the position of the Old Catholics, and, referring to the stance of the Krausists in general, states: "As concerns the disciples of Sanz del Río, almost all of them have ended up in abstract rationalism. Some of us are hoping and searching for something better. The Spanish people's sincere religious sense of the past, ruined and falsified by a regrettable tradition of centuries, has dwindled into the twilight."[14]

The backdrop for this epistolary exchange was a crisis in religion for the Spanish Krausists caused by the conservative radicalization of the hierarchy of the Catholic Church during the papacy of Pius IX. This approach became evident in the rejection of freedom of conscience and independence of reason

that had been proposed in the Syllabus of 1864, as well as in
the approval of the dogma of papal infallibility at the First
Vatican Council, concluded in 1870. Papal dogma reaffirmed
the most hard-line stances of the church, to the detriment of
those who sought an opening up to the currents of modern
culture. More than a matter of sovereignty, the decisive point
of the dogma was to make clear "that the prime authority of
the pope extended also to matters of truth or doctrine and that
no appeal would be possible of the pope's solemn decisions."[15]
This meant that religious truth was seen as one and inar-
guable, extended to all areas of life, was not confined to the
private sphere, and was not susceptible to subjective decisions
or unorthodox beliefs. Many Krausists, Giner de los Ríos
included, who espoused an anti-dogmatic Catholicism compatible with freedom of conscience and religious plurality,
found it impossible to reconcile their faith in freedom, reason,
and progress with the radicalization of the Church and separated from it.[16] José Luis Abellán has shown how important
this moment was in setting the religious tone for later generations of Spanish intellectuals: "The Krausist crisis is historic
because it meant a crisis in the Spanish conscience. From that
moment on, it was no longer fair to identify Spanish thought
with Catholicism, since the exceptions would prove to be
abundant and often involved the highest levels of culture and
philosophy."[17]

In his classic study *Filosofía Social de Krausismo español*
(*Social Philosophy of Spanish Krausism*) Elias Diaz extends
that concurrence on morality to politics, which helps explain
why Krausist philosophy was so well received: its exaltation of
the individual was consistent with the political organicism of
Spanish progressive liberalism and its rejection of excessive
state intervention.[18] Even the political militancy of the men
and women from the Free Teaching Institute was anything but
uniform. Despite the early Institute members' skepticism
regarding "top-down" reforms, the generations that followed

had a more favourable view of political intervention, a view often accompanied by an explicitly socialist approach. In his 1889 prologue to the collected work *Educación y enseñanza* (*Education and Teaching*), Giner de los Ríos makes his skepticism about political action clear, "where it is our belief that great efforts are wasted on obtaining minimal results."[19] Later, Institute members took part in political initiatives and, in the turbulent times of the Second Republic (1931–39), even held government offices. This was the case for the two main Spanish proponents of Dewey's work: Domingo Barnés and Lorenzo Luzuriaga. Barnés was sub-secretary twice between 1931 and 1936 and for a few months was minister of public instruction and fine arts. In that position he had to apply the principle of secular schooling mandated in the Constitution of 1931. Luzuriaga belonged to the Liga de Educación Política Española (Spanish League for Political Education), founded by José Ortega y Gasset and Manuel Azaña in October 1913, and to the Núñez de Arenas New School, which was linked to the Spanish Workers' Socialist Party (PSOE). He was devoted to the socialist ideal of a common, secular, and public school.

This, then, was the intellectual background at the time Dewey and progressive pedagogy were introduced at the Free Teaching Institute. Giner de los Ríos had died in 1915, the same year the first chapter of Dewey's *School and Society* was published in Spain and one year before *Democracy and Education* was published in the United States. Giner de los Ríos was not unaware of Dewey, whom he cited in passing in some of his last writings.[20] His relationship with American pedagogy had started in 1889 when, at the Conference on Education in Paris, he and his Free Teaching Institute colleague Manuel Bartolomé Cossío met William Torrey Harris, who represented the United States Bureau of Education.[21] During that year and the next Cossío wrote a few notes on education in the United States for the Free Teaching Institute's journal, the *Boletín de la Institución Libre de Enseñanza*.[22] A few years later, in 1898, the *Boletín* incorporated extensive extracts from creeds written by recognized American educators that had been published by *The School Journal*, including a practically unabridged version of Dewey's *My Pedagogic Creed*.[23] This was the first translation into Spanish of one of Dewey's works. The *Creed*, whose translator remains anonymous, cannot, however, be considered a contribution that brought knowledge of Dewey to Spain; rather, it was one of many creeds published in *The School Journal*.[24] Dewey's name did not yet trigger the recognition it would acquire in subsequent decades. In the summer of 1904, having recently attained the chair in Higher Pedagogy at the University of Madrid, Cossío, who was aware of the ideas of American progressive education, traveled to the United States for several weeks.[25] He does not seem to have had any direct contact with Dewey, who was preparing to leave Chicago for Columbia University after first making a trip to Europe.[26] But, in a lecture delivered the following year, Cossío referred to that trip and made an appeal for "one of the greatest principles restored by contemporary education: that of 'learning by doing' of the American people." [27] It was the next generations of Institute members, represented by Barnés and Luzuriaga, who would spread Dewey's ideas in Spain, following in the steps of Giner de los Ríos and Cossío and a few pedagogues in Catalonia.[28]

The environment in which Dewey's ideas were received conditioned how those ideas were interpreted. Krausism's moral humanism lead to a softened reading of pragmatism and its invitation to consider "that humanity is an open-ended notion, that the word 'human' names a fuzzy but promising project rather than an essence." [29] Not all Institute members were equally Krausist in thought, but, although the influence of Krause's philosophy began to wane at the turn of the new century, it continued to be influential in readings of Dewey's works. Furthermore, the liberalism of the early Krausists eventually gave way to a belief in the importance of greater political commitment, which led to a more socially and politically oriented reading of Dewey's ideas.

A SOFTENED READING OF DEWEY: DOMINGO BARNÉS

The *Boletín de la Institución Libre de Enseñanza* (*BILE*) was the mouthpiece of the Free Teaching Institute and one of the most significant pedagogic journals of the time. John Dewey was its second favourite author from outside the Spanish-Portuguese linguistic area in terms of the number of translations published (eleven articles between 1915 and 1929), surpassed only by the Belgian Alexis Sluys (around twenty articles) and followed by the Swiss psychologist Édouard Claparède (seven articles) and Michael Ernest Sadler from Britain (six articles).[30] And yet there were only two articles that actually analyzed Dewey's pedagogy.[31] This disparity may have occurred because those involved with the journal were interested primarily in disseminating original works or perhaps were using Dewey to reinforce ideas already known from other sources.

If we eliminate the 1898 version of *My Pedagogic Creed*, the first specific identifiable contribution by Dewey to be translated and published in Spain was the first chapter of *School and Society*, "School and Social Progress," in the May 1915 issue of the *Boletín*.[32] That chapter had been published in 1903 in German in the journal *Zeitschrift für Pädagogische Psychologie*, and in French in 1909 in the journal *l'Éducation*, edited by Georges Bertier, director of l'École des Roches, an institution familiar to those in the Institute. These connections suggest that the way Dewey's pedagogy was interpreted in Spain may have been mediated by other readings of his work.

In a comment on the book Émile Boutroux dedicated to William James in 1911, the Catalonian philosopher Eugeni d'Ors pointed out Boutroux's tendency to "Frenchify" his reading of pragmatism, suggesting that he softened it and suppressed its less friendly side.[33] This softening is discernable, for example, in his attempt at reconciling James with traditional classical reason, even with Descartes.[34] It is also noticeable in the somewhat apologetic reading Boutroux provides of James's pedagogy in the fifth chapter, translated and published that same year in Spain by the *Boletín de la Institución Libre de Enseñanza*.[35] In this chapter, Boutroux argues that it is not that the search for an ideal of life made up of a set of virtues as the aim of education makes no sense for pragmatism. Rather, it is simply not a fitting subject for it. As Boutroux concludes, "certainly, it must be correct to keep posing these questions; but it is not the place of a philosophy of experience and action to seek them out and answer once and for all, as a scientific rationalism would. Life is and shall be a problem, infinite as itself, and that only it may progressively resolve."[36]

The mediator for the reception of Dewey's work in Spain was the psychologist from Geneva, Edouard Claparède. Domingo Barnés had brought Dewey's ideas to Spain, amid the conceptual baggage of Paidology. Barnés belonged to the younger generation of the Free Teaching Institute and, influenced by Claparède's functional psychology, was one of the driving forces behind the scientific study of the child. Claparède had written the introduction to the collected works of Dewey, *L'École et l'Enfant*, perhaps the first study in French of Dewey's pedagogy.[37] Part of this introduction was published in Spanish in the *Boletín de la Institución Libre de Enseñanza*.[38] In it Claparède makes a psycho-pedagogic reading of Dewey centred on three characteristics: genetic, functional, and social. As Daniel Tröhler has shown, however, the three are not all given the same weight in Claparède's reading. The first two, considered together, "are interpreted as one of the core problems of education, while the social aspect is hardly discussed at all. This 'ignoring' of the social dimension accords with the way in which Dewey's educational theory was viewed in 'isolation' from pragmatism." [39]

In his introduction, Claparède tries to establish a certain distance between Dewey and pragmatism. Dewey, writes Claparéde in a footnote, "holds, in any case, a separate place within this movement. He has indicated what distinguishes him from W. James in a review of one of the latter's works." [40] To Claparède, Dewey's pedagogy and psychology could thus be easily separated from their pragmatic trunk. The convenience of separating the psychological and the philosophical aspects of pragmatism, which James himself ironically remarked on, had been proposed five years earlier by the Zurich psychologist and educator Gustav Störring.[41] Claparède accepts this separation, saying:

> Dewey has also, from the point of view of pragmatism, taken on the important domain of education, and nowhere else does pragmatism seem to have such a beautiful fertility; if applied to morality and logic, it raises certain difficulties that many thinkers cannot accept, but here, it seems to assemble all the impartial minds.
>
> But let us forget pragmatism. Dewey's psycho-pedagogy, though a faithful expression of it, is in no way bound to the fate of this doctrine. Dewey himself does not use the word even once in all of his work on education, which could just as easily have been conceived by a psychologist or biologist who had never concerned himself with questions of theoretical philosophy.[42]

Barnés kept in close contact with Claparède and with the J.J. Rousseau Institute that the latter had founded. Many of the works of the Rousseau Institute were translated and published in Spanish through Barnés's influence. Barnés attended its courses and was a force behind the creation of the Spanish

Association of Friends of the Rousseau Institute in Madrid.[43]
He translated several of Claparède's books: *La asociación de las
ideas* (*Association of Ideas*, 1907) and the third and eighth editions of *Psicología del niño y Pedagogía experimental* (*Child
Psychology and Experimental Pedagogy*, 1911 and 1927).
Another result of that relationship was the publication of a
number of Claparède's articles in the BILE and in the *Revista de
Pedagogía*, including an extract from the lectures given in 1923
at the National Pedagogic Museum in Madrid, of which Barnés
was secretary.[44] Claparède's influence was apparent in successive re-editions of Barnés's main work, *Paidología*, which had
resulted from his doctoral dissertation, presented in 1904. The
evolution of the various editions of the text shows a move
toward greater functionalism and "a distancing from the
German child psychology that had previously exerted more
influence on his work."[45] While the original text of 1904 barely
mentioned Claparède, by the 1932 edition he was the fourth
most-cited author, after Johann Heinrich Pestalozzi, Jean-
Jacques Rousseau, and Johann Friedrich Herbart and immediately above Dewey.[46] According to Rosa M. Cardá and Helio
Carpintero, this third edition also reveals a greater interest in
the social aspect, due, in their opinion, to the influence of the
American philosopher.[47]

Barnés was also one of the chief disseminators of Dewey and
pragmatism in Spain. He translated William James's *Principles
of Psychology*[48] and wrote an article on the pedagogy of pragmatism.[49] He was also responsible for publication in Spain of
the first translated text by Dewey, "School and Social
Progress." This text was part of the complete Spanish edition
of Dewey's *School and Society*, which Barnés translated and
for which he wrote a prologue.[50] In his prologue, Barnés
focuses on Claparède's interpretation of Dewey's pedagogy,
which Claparède summarized as genetic, functional, and
social. Barnés particularly emphasized the social aspect:
preparing for life in society is what gives meaning to the learn-

ing by doing methodology. To Barnés, emphasis on the social is a feature common to all American pedagogy, and an idea first stated by Froebel:

> To American pedagogy, moral education must get its inspiration in a broad social sense. What they call "new education" is an intense flowering of trends and works to purify all social life. In this movement influenced by Pestalozzi and Herbart, Froebel is the first to suggest an evolutionary principle of education, one that involves not only faith in the environment as a suitable corrective to pernicious inheritance but also several other corollaries applicable to education, one of the most important of which is the doctrine of solidarity.[51]

According to Barnés, "to the French pedagogues, this social character is the most typical aspect of Dewey's pedagogy."[52] In reality, the social side of Dewey's pedagogy seems to have been of more interest to the Spanish author than to his French counterparts. In both countries, the first chapter of *School and Society* was used to introduce Dewey's ideas. The brief presentation accompanying the French edition explains the reason this text was translated as: "We find it of interest to publish it at the time when the introduction of handiwork in our schools is raising passionate discussions."[53] In comparison with this more methodologically oriented reading, Barnés's reading, as taken from his prologue to the book, points from the start toward more interest in the social.

In 1926, Barnés translated and also wrote the prologue to a collection of Dewey's articles under the title *La escuela y el niño* (*The School and the Child*),[54] partially based on the collection edited by J.L. Findlay in England.[55] In it, Barnés refers again to Claparède's characterization. He argues that pragmatism is best understood as a method of investigation rather than a philosophical stance and says that "Claparède is right in stating that, although Dewey's psycho-pedagogy is the faithful expression of pragmatism, its fate is by no means bound to the fate of that doctrine. And it is odd and symptomatic that Dewey does not even name it in any of his philosophic works."[56] The separation of Dewey's pedagogy from its pragmatic roots leads Barnés to a transcendentalist reading of Dewey in which *growth* becomes *self-fulfillment*.[57] This conversion allows him to link Dewey's pedagogy with Krausian philosophy, for whom "fulfilling one's own essence was also the ethical purpose of the individual,"[58] and with Rousseauian naturalism. Regarding the latter, Barnés states that "the first thing a child should be prepared for, says Rousseau, is to carry out his mission of becoming fully human. Dewey would agree with these words, adding only the caveat that human beings are social beings and only in society, in action and reaction with it, can they accomplish their mission and destiny."[59]

This reading requires re-adjusting Dewey's notion of education as growth and reconstruction of experience, in which there exists no external end guiding the process, no essence to realize, no destiny to fulfill. As Oelkers points out, Dewey retained the term "growth" but gave it a radically different meaning from the one it had had in previous pedagogical theories, one that "removes itself from the organic concept of growth on the one hand and from finalistic conceptions of development on the other."[60] In *Democracy and Education*, by then published in Spain, Dewey distinguishes his view from that of the unfolding of the absolute ideal in G.W.F. Hegel and Froebel. Regarding the latter's contributions to education, so highly valued by the Spanish institutionists, he writes:

Froebel's recognition of the significance of the native capacities of children, his loving attention to them, and his influence in inducing others to study them, represent perhaps the most effective single force in modern educational theory in effecting widespread acknowledgment of the idea of growth.

But his formulation of the notion of development and his organization of devices for promoting it were badly hampered by the fact that he conceived development to be the unfolding of a ready-made latent principle. He failed to see that growing is growth, developing is development, and consequently placed the emphasis upon the completed product. Thus he set up a goal which meant the arrest of growth, and a criterion which is not applicable to immediate guidance of powers, save through translation into abstract and symbolic formulae.[61]

In the 1926 prologue to *School and the Child*, Barnés kept some distance from Claparède, whose reading of Dewey's pedagogy he considered a bit limited. This pedagogy, he stated, is social "and not only because it is functional, but because of all its characteristics."[62] Barnés refers to Dewey's article "Democracy and Education," published in Monroe's *Cyclopedia of Education,* in order to emphasize that his pedagogy was not only social but democratic. This democratic meaning, he explains, does not end at stressing the need to teach citizens how to live in a political system in which they are the lawmakers. There is another dimension, more diffuse and vague but effective nonetheless, which affects school behaviour both in its organization and in the form and content of its teaching.[63]

Barnés is touching on what is perhaps Dewey's most genuine contribution to pedagogy: the intimate tie between education and democracy. This link is not limited to the recognition that education should prepare people to take part in social institutions, which constitutes the "political and more external relation of democracy to education."[64] Beyond that external relation there is a deeper one. Democracy inevitably leads to greater respect for the individual, to increased initiative-taking and autonomy, and to a heightened concern for others and for the commitments this concern requires. "Insensibly, rather than consciously, the atmosphere characteristic of democracy pene-

trates school methods and materials and modifies educational
ideals."[65] From the point of view of a kind of knowledge that
renounces any a priori truth and directional end beyond one's
own experience, education can only be democratic, and democracy can only be sustained through education. As Johnston
points out, in Dewey this interrelation reached maturity with
the publication of *Democracy and Education*.[66] In his prologue,
Barnés announced the upcoming appearance of the Spanish
translation of this book.[67]

PARALLEL READINGS OF DEWEY:
LORENZO LUZURIAGA

Lorenzo Luruziaga was in charge of the project that resulted in
the translation of *Democracy and Education* into Spanish and
its publication in several volumes by *La Lectura* in 1926 and
1927, during the dictatorship of Primo de Rivera.[68] Luzuriaga
was ten years younger than Barnés. According to Herminio Barreiro, he had three main sources of inspiration: the proponents
of the Free Teaching Institute, where he had been a student and
a teacher; Ortega y Gasset, who introduced him to German philosophy and culture; and socialist militancy.[69] He was closely
tied to the New Education movement, about which he wrote
several books and whose conferences he assiduously attended.
He was also a member of the International Committee of the
New Education League and a delegate in the International Education Office. His books, articles, and translations greatly aided
the spread of pedagogical ideas and movements for innovation.
To that end, in 1922 he created the journal *Revista de Pedagogía*, using the money he and his wife had saved to buy winter
coats. Dewey was one of his favourite writers along with Kerschensteiner, Paul Natorp, Eduard Spranger, Roger Cousinet,
and Decroly.[70]

In 1918, in his customary column in the newspaper *El Sol*,
edited by Ortega y Gasset, Luzuriaga published his first article

on Dewey's pedagogy under the title "La educación por la acción" (Education through Action). This seminal article was meant to introduce readers to new pedagogical theories from abroad, going beyond ideas from Germany, which had traditionally predominated in Spain. Regarding pragmatism, Luzuriaga states that "this is not the place, nor is it my competence, to explain what pragmatism is."[71] Aside from the fact that neither the type of publication nor Luzuriaga's limited knowledge of philosophy allowed him to delve any deeper in pragmatism, epistemological problems were not his top priority. He was mainly a man of action and was committed to theory as a basis for action. This focus meant that eventually Luzuriaga's reading of Dewey would take on a more political, less transcendental nature. It has been claimed that Luzuriaga was a peculiar institutionist: born to a family of teachers, he was not the prototypical Free Teaching Institute student, who generally came from the reform-minded bourgeoisie. From early in his youth, he frequented circles of socialist workers and like-minded organizations, such as the New School of Núñez de Arenas, which advocated intellectual and vocational training for workers. The same year his seminal article on Dewey was published in *El Sol*, Luzuriaga was preparing his *Bases para un programa de instrucción pública (Bases for a Program of Public Instruction)*, which the Núñez de Arenas organization then presented at the Conference of the Spanish Workers' Socialist Party.[72]

In presenting Dewey to the public, Luzuriaga stressed what in his opinion constituted one of Dewey's greatest contributions: "That we can represent synthetically with the formula of the school as society and of 'education through action' in which it can be resolved."[73] Despite the ambiguous wording, "education through action" here seems to abandon an exclusively psychological meaning. The focus is no longer only on the child's needs but on the school as a microcosm of society. School activities must therefore be seen not as leading to special skills, nor as vocational training, but as "instruments by which the school aspires to be a genuine form of active communal life."[74] The article closes with a fragment presented under the title "La educación mediante el trabajo" (Education through Work), taken from chapter 10, "Education through Industry," of Dewey's *Schools of Tomorrow*, which Luzuriaga had just translated for publication in Spain.[75] As on other occasions, the publication of his translation was preceded by publication of a chapter in the *Boletín de la Institución Libre de Enseñanza*.[76] It is this aspect of Dewey's contribution that Luzuriaga chose to use to introduce him to a Spanish audience.

In 1925, Luzuriaga dedicated a second work to Dewey, his preface to the Spanish edition of *The Child and the Curriculum*. His discussion focused once again on Claparède, of whom he says that, with the exception of his study – probably alluding to the preface to *L'école et l'énfant* – "we do not know any other work on Dewey's complete pedagogy."[77] To Claparède's three distinguishing elements, Luzuriaga adds three more: activity, vitality, and acknowledgement of childhood personality. His treatment of Dewey is much like Barnés's at that period. This reading ended up dominating the more socio-political approach suggested in his presentation of *Schools of Tomorrow*. In the preface to *The Child and the Curriculum*, Luzuriaga states that, in addition to Claparède's work, his main sources for Dewey's ideas are *School and Society* and *My Pedagogic Creed*.[78] *Schools of Tomorrow*, which he had translated several years earlier, and *Democracy and Education*, about to be published in his translation, seem to have been overlooked. This second work on Dewey belongs to what has been called the "professional" period of Luzuriaga's career, which Barreiro contrasts with the more political orientation of his previous period (1914 to 1921), an orientation to which he returned in the days of the Second Republic.[79]

The methodological aspect of the activity principle takes a predominant role in his readings of Dewey in this second work. Luzuriaga bases his interpretation on the work of the German pedagogue Kerschensteiner. He writes that "John Dewey may in fact be considered one of the creators of the modern 'active school.' No one else comes close to his defence of the principle of activity at school, an interpretation that coincides with Kerschensteiner's conception of the 'work school.'"[80] Luzuriaga had learned of Kerschensteiner's pedagogy when he was in Germany in 1913 and 1914 and some of his articles on the work school published at the time suggest this potential influence on his reading of Dewey.[81] Luzuriaga often insisted on the similarities between the two authors. In 1918 he wrote an article on Kerschensteiner, publishing it in *El Sol* and later including it in the *Boletín de la Institución Libre de Enseñanza*. In it he argues that both authors, along with Maria Montessori, constitute the corner points of the "voluntarist trend in education, although each has his own understanding of it."[82] He glosses over the differences between them, stating that "Dewey highlights above all the instrumental, pragmatic – not utilitarian – concept of education, and Kerschensteiner the professional and social one."[83] In the 1920s, Luzuriaga asked Kerschensteiner to write an article for the *Revista de Pedagogía*,[84] and Luzuriaga himself translated *Der Begriff der Arbeitsschule (The Concept of the Work School)* and *Das Problem der Volkserziehung (The Problem of National Education)*.[85] For this latter translation, he wrote another piece on the German pedagogue. In it, he again considers Dewey to be the "partner figure" of Kerschensteiner, in part because both advocate the fusion of theory and practice in education.[86]

Kerschensteiner had expressed his admiration for Dewey, whom he met personally in 1910. At a speech on the work school, given in 1908 at St Peter's Church in Zurich to commemorate Pestalozzi, he offered "the well-known philosopher of Columbia University" as an example of the activity principle and child-centred pedagogy. In a footnote in the printed version of this speech, he referred to *School and Society*, saying: "I should like most heartily to recommend to all teachers this book, which first came into my hands in 1907."[87] However, Philipp Gonon maintains that Kerschensteiner read Dewey apolitically, a position that he associates with Kerschensteiner's ambivalence to the American philosopher and to pragmatism. Kerschensteiner expressly demonstrates this position in a letter in which he told Spranger: "You need not be afraid that Dewey and his pragmatism could get a hold on me." The reading of James, stated Kirschensteiner flatly in the letter, meant nothing to him, and as for Dewey, he acknowledged being in debt to his clarity "in almost everything which *I myself* wanted and instinctively strove for."[88]

An apolitical reading of Dewey cannot be similarly claimed for Luzuriaga, who translated *Democracy and Education*, which he came to consider a pivotal work in the history of education.[89] In the *Revista de Pedagogía*, especially in its later period during the Spanish Second Republic, Luzuriaga disseminated this more political side of Dewey, and did so in a way that led to Dewey's ideas being more quickly received than had been the case in earlier decades. The last two works by Dewey published before the journal was closed in 1936 were "Education and Our Present Social Problems," a lecture delivered by Dewey at the Department of Supervisors and Directors of Instruction of the National Education Association (Minneapolis, March 1933)[90] and "The Future of Liberalism," an address at the twenty-fourth annual meeting of the American Philosophical Association (New York City, December 1934).[91]

Luzuriaga's changing interpretations seem to be the result of difficulties in deciding how to integrate the various readings of Dewey. An example of this can be seen in his treatment of ideas of the unique or unified school and the work or active school. He began to develop these ideas during his time in Germany, using the concepts of *Einheitsschule* and *Arbeit-*

schule. In an article written during his stay he says, "The so-called 'unique school' is nothing less than a school large enough to combine all current teaching institutions, from kindergarten on. This school would put an end to the heterogeneity and irregularity rampant in today's educational institutions – differences which exist only for purely historical reasons – and would combine primary school, secondary school, and university into one large graduated whole made up of those very institutions."[92] Luzuriaga distinguishes this idea from the idea of the work school, about which he says, in another article written in Germany: "Unlike that conception of the unique school – that great, graduated school that encompasses and unifies all the current teaching institutions – and mainly refers to how the teaching institution is organised outwardly, the conception of the school as a workplace addresses the core of education, the intimate life of the school. Both ideas are reciprocal and complementary, and together cover the whole range of educational endeavour."[93] In 1931, summarizing his position, Luzuriaga insisted again:

> There are two basic concepts in education today: "unique school" and "active school." The "unique school" is a socio-pedagogic concept, a new concept in school organization that must be understood as an "external form of organization." It is a social movement advocated by the most advanced political parties and is a growing reaction by the popular political parties and public primary school teachers. The "active school" is a psycho-pedagogic concept referring to the content and internal life of the educational institutions.[94]

For Luzuriaga, the two concepts are complementary but do not actually interact. They refer to two separate realities of schooling. The active school is a methodological concept, whereas the unique or unified school is a political and organi-

zational concept that addresses the need to unite the different
grades, thereby breaking the dual structure of a primary education for the masses and a secondary and higher education
restricted to the elite.[95] However, by splitting the active school
and the unified school into two dissociated realities, Luzuriaga
separates what for Dewey necessarily go together on a
methodological or organizational level as well as on a conceptual one. For Dewey, a unified school also means an active
school, in the sense that for him the unity of schoolwork refers
not only to the need to adapt to the continuum of life, without
any artificial barriers, as they did at the Laboratory School,[96]
but also to the continuity of intellectual work and manual
work, whose separation he felt was the result of the old social
structure of class division.[97] The need for this continuity is a
consequence of the pragmatic postulate that thought and
action must be joined and is what would have allowed
Luzuriaga to integrate the notions of unified school and active
school into a whole that is at the same time pedagogical and
political.

Luzuriaga had to leave Spain during the Spanish Civil War.
Once in exile, he sent Dewey a signed copy of his book *Historia de la Educación Pública (History of Public Education)*.[98] In
it he says that he considers Dewey to be "the most eminent
defender of educational democratization in our time. His fundamental work in fact bears the title *Democracy and Education*.
In it, he expounds his essential pedagogical theories in parallel
to his conception of democratic education."[99] To Luzuriaga, the
concept of democratic education is *parallel* to Dewey's contributions to pedagogy. The two issues are separate, like two parallel lines. A bit further on, considering the situation in Spanish
pedagogy, Luzuriaga adds: "In the purely theoretical aspect,
and referring to our times, the first manifestations in favour of
democratizing education and of the unique school were those of
the author of this book, who in 1914 reported on the German
Einheitsschule movement and disseminated the ideas of demo-

cratic education in various periodicals."[100] Here, democracy refers exclusively to an external organizational dimension of the school system, motivated by the aspiration to provide "all men with the most education they are capable of, whatever their social and economic standing."[101] Democracy here is not an internal dimension of schoolwork, which involves, as Dewey indicated, a "modification of traditional ideals of culture, traditional subjects of study and traditional methods of teaching and discipline."[102]

The separation of political and pedagogical readings of Dewey is one indication that the public school – which Luzuriaga so strenuously advocated – had become subordinated to an external goal, which Dewey analyzed in chapter 7 of *Democracy and Education* in relation to the nationalistic orientation of the German education system and pedagogical theory in the nineteenth century. Dewey felt that because of this subordination the public service aspect of education was confused with the purpose of that education. To Dewey, democracy is not an end imposed on education from the outside, a fixed goal that must be reached. Rather, he believes it to be a criterion for action. In chapter 8, "Aims in Education" in *Democracy and Action*, Dewey states that "until the democratic criterion of the intrinsic significance of every growing experience is recognized, we shall be intellectually confused by the demand for adaptation to external aims."[103] Dewey's theory is based on a "metaphysics of experience."[104] Experience provides an active sense of self-creating growth that develops through social interaction. This is the core of the Deweyan concept of democracy. From a pragmatic point of view, democracy cannot be an ideal outside experience. Democracy consists of "a mode of associated living, of conjoint communicated experience."[105] Similarly, education is not a set of activities carried out to reach some goal separate from them, but "a constant reorganizing or reconstructing of experience."[106] This sense of experience constantly being reorganized is the meaning of the activity principle when it is understood as a force of growth rather than a drive for development or the unfolding of something latent. The activity principle is not a simple methodological principle but provides the gears that are essential to connect education and democracy. That connection, said Dewey, is based on a philosophy of education in which education is seen "as a freeing of individual capacity in a progressive growth directed to social aims. Otherwise a democratic criterion of education can only be inconsistently applied."[107]

In Luzuriaga, the readings of Dewey overlap without interacting. Dewey is inserted into a pedagogical project and provides support for a political goal, but his work is not strictly interpreted as part of a body of a particular philosophy. There is no pedagogical and political theory based strictly on Dewey's ideas, but only partial readings of his works in conjunction with many other readings. Luzuriaga may have learned about Dewey the philosopher through one of his teachers, Ortega y Gasset, whom he had greatly admired ever since his student days at the Escuela Superior del Magisterio (Higher School of Teaching) in Madrid.[108] Yet this potential line of access to Dewey was eventually closed: in the foreword to the French edition of *La revolución de las masas* (*The Revolt of the Masses*), Ortega y Gasset boasted retrospectively that, when others were fascinated by the American mirage, he had maintained that the Americas, especially North America, "far from being the future, was actually a far-off past because it meant primitivism."[109] For him, pragmatism was a kind of backfill philosophy that had taken advantage of the leaderless interval between the decline of neo-Kantism and the apex of phenomenology.[110] The presence of this movement did not call into question the predominance of German philosophy: "There have been things initiated or carried out to perfection outside Germany – an example of the first being American pragmatism; of the second, mathematical logic – but they did not produce any decisive, operant philosophical effect, they were not full reality, that is to say, they were not *vis historica* until they were integrated into the framework of German thought."[111] Perhaps that is why, even though Ortega y Gasset's vitalism is not far from some of the theses of pragmatism, he never cited Dewey and barely mentioned Charles Sanders Peirce and James.[112]

From Ortega y Gasset's point of view, the great admiration for Dewey's pedagogy compared with the secondary place of pragmatism in philosophy would come to prove the *anachronism* the Spanish philosopher believed was congenital to pedagogical knowledge.[113] Ortega y Gasset was a philosopher. Luzuriaga, in contrast, was moved more by a social and political commitment. Epistemological discussion interested him less than the support Dewey's ideas could provide to a project for education and society. He took from Dewey, as Kerschensteiner said in his letter to Spranger, what he *himself* was already seeking.

AMBIVALENCE TO PRAGMATISM

In Spain, Dewey's reception lacked the element of personal contact that it had in other contexts. Despite being well known by 1925, there is no record that he had any sort of academic relation or contact with Spanish pedagogues, particularly those of the Free Teaching Institute, during his visit to Madrid in June of that year as part of his trip around Europe with Albert C. Barnes.[114] During the years of the Spanish Civil War (1936–39), Dewey took an active interest in the political events unfolding in the country but not in its education. He was chairman and vice-chairman of the American Friends of Spanish Democracy. In 1937 he published his famous letter in *The Christian Century* refuting arguments by those who opposed sending aid or recruiting American volunteers to support the government of the Republic.[115] The following year, at the instigation of Franz Boas, he signed the "Open Letter on Culture

and Democracy in Spain" to protest the execution of Leopoldo
Alas and other Spanish intellectuals.[116] Aside from a few letters
from the same period, motivated by political circumstances,
there was no consolidated exchange of mail of a scholarly
nature with Spanish intellectuals. Dewey's presence was distant
and impersonal.

Nevertheless, despite that distance, Dewey's ideas resonated
in Spain because they agreed with the aspirations of the times.
Rather than a revolution, his pedagogical ideas represented a
reaffirmation of a number of prior intuitions that had been
combined in the activity principle advocated by Free Teaching
Institute members, building on the pedagogy of Froebel. Thus it
comes as no surprise that in 1917 Eugeni D'Ors tried to show
the common elements in Froebel and Dewey through the philosophy of Fichte.[117] Dewey himself referred to Froebel on
several different occasions as a predecessor – or re-discoverer,
after Plato – in recognizing the pedagogical value of activity and
play, but he also pointed out the distance that separated his
ideas from Froebel's romantic or symbolic idealism. To Dewey,
Froebel's symbolism was due to the lack of knowledge of the
physiological and psychological principles of child growth at
the time, and to the social and political circumstances of the
German nation, which made it impossible to conceive of any
continuity between the free, cooperative life of kindergarten and
life in the outside world.[118]

In *Democracy and Education*, Dewey wrote: "The conception that growth and progress are just approximations to a
final unchanging goal is the last infirmity of the mind in its
transition from a static to a dynamic understanding of life."[119]
The distance separating both understandings of life is pragmatism. Once the distrust resulting from the military defeat of
1898 had been overcome, pragmatism had an effect on Spanish
authors such as Eugeni D'Ors and Miguel de Unamuno.
James's works were welcomed early on.[120] But it was a
nuanced reception. The ambivalence felt by the Free Teaching

Institute members toward pragmatic philosophy are revealed in a letter D'Ors, considered its main proponent in Spain, sent to Giner de los Ríos in 1909. In it, the Catalonian philosopher excused himself to Giner de los Ríos, explaining: "I am not a pragmatist in the strictest sense of the word, as you seem to fear, although like any other man who deals today with matters of understanding, I am constantly having to deal with Pragmatism."[121] D'Ors considered that James's pragmatism had two main limits. First, he thought James's epistemological theory should be complemented by Schiller's aesthetic approach. Second D'Ors felt, unlike James, that religious sentiment could not be considered a primary phenomenon but must be seen as a symbol of a deeper reality. D'Ors had explored the epistemological and religious aspects of James's work in two different papers presented at the Third International Congress on Philosophy held in Heidelberg in 1908, at which pragmatism was widely discussed.[122] George Fullerton, however does not mention either of the two papers in his summary of the Congress sessions published in *The Journal of Philosophy, Psychology and Scientific Methods.*[123] Spain was apparently not considered relevant in the context of that discussion.

Yet Spain was not unfertile ground for pragmatism. Spanish philosophy at the turn of the nineteenth to twentieth century had been characterized by the ambivalence between idealism and pragmatism.[124] Moreover, references to the philosophy upheld by the Free Teaching Institute used the expression *pragmatic rationalism.*[125] Although the appeal to pragmatism in this context sometimes alludes more to a general stance than to adherence to the philosophical movement initiated by Peirce, these characterizations reveal a propitious climate for this philosophy. D'Ors ended his letter to Giner de los Ríos by stating: "You, my dear professor, cannot be an anti-pragmatist. The harmonious Spaniard[126] could triumphantly make claim to some of the points of view being unravelled today by pragmatism. There would be something well worth vindicating on that side."[127] It cannot be claimed that the Institute members were anti-pragmatic in the same way as Albert Schinz, whose position, as can be seen from by D'Ors's comments, was to neither his nor Giner de los Ríos's liking.[128]

As intellectuals of the time, the representatives of the Free Teaching Institute clearly displayed the attitude James referred to in his lectures in 1906 and 1907, that of those who "want a system that will combine both things, the scientific loyalty to facts and willingness to take account of them, the spirit of adaptation and accommodation, in short, but also the old confidence in human values and the resultant spontaneity, whether of the religious or the romantic type."[129] James's answer to the tension between what he called tough-minded and tender-minded temperaments was pragmatism; the Spanish institutionists' answer was so-called "Krausopositivism," an attempted reconciliation of experience and reason, with which it was hoped, in the words of the Krausist Nicolás Salmerón, "to rectify the old dualism which has made Physics and Metaphysics hostile and reciprocally deficient ... This way will settle the historical contradiction between empiricism and idealism, without forgetting or annulling either of the two essential elements for scientific construction."[130]

With reference to the tension between empiricism and idealism, which James described, Dewey's pragmatism leaned toward the empirical world. For that reason, as John Childs pointed out, for Dewey something as subjective as the satisfaction gained from religious experience could not be considered proof of truth, which differed from what James held in that regard.[131] In *Religion and Our Schools*, Dewey called for a type of naturalized religious education consistent with a democratic lifestyle and modern science, subject to the same criteria for proof required in any other field of knowledge. Consequently, he advocated that, until the non-supernatural dynamics of nature, the world, and human beings were better known, the role of the school in religious education should be restricted as much as possible so as not to hinder the budding of a new form of religion which would accord with the modern spirit, which for him was science and democracy:

> It may be that the symptoms of religious ebb as convention-ally interpreted are symptoms of the coming of a fuller and deeper religion. I do not claim to know. But of one thing I am quite sure: our ordinary opinions about the rise and falling off of religion are highly conventional, based mostly upon the acceptance of a standard of religion which is the product of just those things in historic religions which are ceasing to be credible. So far as education is concerned, those who believe in religion as a natural expression of human experience must devote themselves to the develop-ment of the ideas of life which lie implicit in our still new science and our still newer democracy. They must interest themselves in the transformation of those institutions which still bear the dogmatic and the feudal stamp (and which do not?) till they are in accord with these ideas. In performing this service, it is their business to do what they can to prevent all public educational agencies from being employed in ways which inevitably impede the recognition of the spiri-tual import of science and of democracy, and hence of that type of religion which will be the fine flower of the modern spirit's achievement.[132]

For the Spanish institutionists, the balance between tough-minded and tender-minded temperaments (to use James's terms) shifted in the other direction in different ways. They tried to combine Darwin's evolutionism with Krause's rationalism,[133] that is, as James would say, the intimacy of facts and the possi-bility of salvation.[134] In a note to his essay "Science as a Social Function" Giner de los Ríos wrote: "The theories of inheritance, whether in the Darwinian sense or in the sense of Weismann and others, strive to explain the problem of individuality as a product of pre-existing empirical factors, leaving aside the conception of what may be called transcendental individuality (Leibnitz, Krause)."[135] Giner de los Ríos wished to save mankind from being captured by a world that consisted only of empirical facts. And he did so by using Krause. Krause's philosophy was self-defined as panentheist, a stance that hoped to reconcile theism with pantheism. James referred to the latter as the last refuge for theists once Darwinism is accepted, a theory that suppresses the idea of design and thus the root of radical, dogmatic theism[136] "still taught rigorously in the seminaries of the Catholic Church."[137] The institutionists fought against this dogmatism and advocated a neutral education, which set them against the Catholic Church. Yet their pedagogical project required an ideal of human development that went beyond empirical conditions. This ideal explains the softened, transcendental reading of Dewey's pedagogy, shorn from its philosophical root, as seen in Barnés.[138]

In 1948, on the occasion of the Mexican publication of the translation of *Experience and Nature*, José Gaos, Ortega y Gasset's disciple who had been exiled to Mexico by the dictatorship in Spain, lamented the lack of interest in translating Dewey's philosophical works into Spanish that had existed for years. He took this lack of interest as a great failing, since Dewey's pragmatism presented a challenge for settling the philosophic problem of modernity, which to Gaos boiled down to the problem of the relationship between immanence and transcendence. Dewey, as Gaos pointed out, tried to bridge the gap between these two worlds by naturalizing mankind and God.[139] For the Spanish institutionists, embedded as they were in European culture, this solution perhaps went too far. In consequence, they went only halfway in their reading of pragmatism. Barnés, in a piece in 1920 on the philosophy of values, read pragmatism as a way of replacing naturalist positivism with a humanist positivism, which to his mind made it akin to the European movements (humanistic pragmatism, philosophy of values, and action philosophy) that strove to put "the human spirit in front of the world by imposing human values."[140] The various responses to this aspiration were not, however, equally satisfying. To Barnés, this answer demanded something more than a humanism that "does not aim to uplift what is human by looking in it for the divine."[141] In his opinion, any humanism that understood human values in an empirical rather than ideal sense was insufficient support for education:

Instead of seeking out humanity in History and in Sociology, that is, instead of looking for the reality humankind has created, and working towards an education that can offer that reality as a model and bind future generations to it, Humanism should seek in human beings what is permanent yet evolving: their spirit; more attentive, in their ascendant drive, to the future than to the past. For it is their function in life to foresee that future, their projection in it, the ongoing trial with perfectible reality, their tendency of being the only finite beings capable of striving for the infinite.[142]

In his commentary on pantheism, James added that it is difficult for fact-lovers to assimilate it. "It is dapper, it is noble in the bad sense, in the sense in which to be noble is to be inapt for humble service."[143] The growing commitment to dealing with ground-level social problems forced the institutionists into a more empirically minded stance, which kept them from settling into the "moral holiday" of belief in the Absolute, "to let the world wag its own way, feeling that its issues are in better hands than ours and are none of our business."[144] As the twentieth century developed, the discussion on epistemological problems was increasingly left behind, eclipsed by the predominating concern for social and political issues. This evolution can be seen in Luzuriaga's reading of Dewey.

On 28 August 1942, Luzuriaga replied to Dewey's letter congratulating him on the publication of his book *Pedagogía contemporánea* (*Contemporary Pedagogy*), which the Spanish author had probably sent to Dewey. In his reply, Luzuriaga expressed interest in Dewey's pedagogical ideas and asked permission to translate *Education Today* into Spanish. The letter closes with praise of the liberal spirit of American education, which Luzuriaga considered crucial at that point in history. "I shall continue the diffusion of your educational theories, and those held by your liberal colleagues in the United States, for I believe them to be those most suited to this critical moment in the world's history."[145] Luzuriaga carried out this task in Argentina. Spain had by then taken a different course.

CONCLUSION

In his address delivered in October 1929 in the auditorium of the Horace Mann School of Teachers College as part of the celebration of Dewey's seventieth birthday, I.L. Kandel said: "It is significant that more of Dewey's educational works have been translated than his contributions to pure philosophy."[146] The reception Dewey's ideas had in Spain is a clear example of that imbalance. The Dewey that interested Spanish thinkers was not Dewey the philosopher, but the Dewey who was more immediately useful for modernizing education, the Dewey of functional psychology and learning by doing. Even though the historical circumstances perhaps favoured a more social and political reading than in other countries, Dewey's thought was stripped from its philosophical bases. In *Experience and Education*, Dewey reacted against that reading, arguing that his pedagogy is more a philosophy of education to be proved by experience than a set of teaching practices:

I think that only slight acquaintance with the history of education is needed to prove that educational reformers and innovators alone have felt the need for a philosophy of education. Those who adhered to the established system needed merely a few fine-sounding words to justify existing practices. The real work was done by habits which were so fixed as to be institutional. The lesson for progressive education is that it requires in an urgent degree, a degree more pressing than was incumbent upon former innovators, a philosophy of education based upon a philosophy of experience.[147]

If that is so, any attempt to appropriate a philosophy of education not born of experience results in contradiction. As in any attempt at transposing one experience to another, the receiver will always get only an impure understanding of the other's experience, since it will be mixed with elements of his/her own context. This impure understanding also affected how the Spanish institutionists read Dewey in their attempt to reconcile modern science with a transcendental view of education.

The difficulty of integrating the new ideas and ways of seeing the world that had been introduced by science into pre-existing mental constructs was not unknown to Dewey, who had already written in his article "The Influence of Darwinism on Philosophy" in 1909 that "old ideas give way slowly; for they are more than abstract logical forms and categories. They are habits, predispositions, deeply ingrained attitudes of aversion and preference."[148] Years later the sociologist Norbert Elias, in his classic book *Über den Prozess der Zivilisation*, treated these mental habits as configurations that grow and change in interaction with social structures.[149] This concept of configuration makes it possible to emphasize the dynamic nature of the interaction between the international traffic of ideas and the contexts of its reception, and to understand the latter as active contexts of re-accommodation. In the Spanish case, Barnés and Luzuriaga looked at Dewey, along with many others, through the eyes of those who needed resources to support a pedagogical, social, and political project, even if re-accommodating Dewey's ideas to pre-existing circumstances and mental habits in Spain required cutting them off from a strong sense of pragmatism, as was Barnés's case, or forgetting about pragmatism entirely, as Luzuriaga did. Dewey's peda-gogy was thus enmeshed in what we may call a kaleidoscopic configuration of imprecise limits where authors and trends came together and were cemented by the wish to regenerate society through education.

In Spain, Dewey's influence was not the result of direct per-sonal contact but of his works, which were available to anyone who wished to take what he or she needed. Sometimes they came second-hand, having already been read and interpreted in other contexts. It comes as no surprise that Dewey reacted against the degradation of his pedagogy. Every shift of ideas involves introducing a degree of triviality, as Ortega y Gasset remarked:

> Those who do not know what ingredients "ideas" are made of believe it easy to transfer them from one place and time to another. Not known is that the most lively part on "ideas" is not what one thinks openly and consciously upon thinking them, but rather, what one *underthinks* beneath them, what is assumed as understood when making use of them. These ingredients, invisible and hidden from view, are often experiences of a nation shaped over thousands of years. This *fonde latente* of ideas that sustains, fills, and nurtures them cannot be transferred, as nothing is that is authentic human life. Life is always non-transferable. That is the Fate of history.
>
> Integral transportation of "ideas" is thus illusory. Only

the stalk and the flower are moved, and perhaps, dangling from the branches, the fruit from that year —whatever in them might be immediately useful at that time – but the living part of "ideas," the roots, remain behind in the land of their origin.[150]

The Spanish institutionists picked the flower and the stalk of Dewey's pedagogical ideas and mixed them with other flowers and stalks to make small, multi-hued bouquets. But they left behind the root. A long tradition of thought prevented them from accepting a hard reading of pragmatism. Looking at Dewey's reception in Spain provides an excellent example of how prior configurations enable new ideas to be re-worked but also impose a limit on the way such ideas can be read.

NOTES

1 Cfr. Jean Louis Guereña, "Infancia y Escolarización," in *Historia de la Infancia en la España Contemporánea*, ed. J.M. Borrás (Madrid: Ministerio de Trabajo y Asuntos Sociales 1996), 347–418; and Jean Louis Guereña, "La Educación Popular a Comienzos del Siglo XX," in *La Educación en España a Examen (1898–1998)*, vol. 2, ed. Julio Ruiz Berrio et al. (Madrid: Ministerio de Educación y cultura 1999), 13–34.

2 M. Mar del Pozo, "Channels by which the International Pedagogic Movement of the New School Spread throughout Spain (1889–1936)," in *Conference Papers for the 9th Session of the International Standing Conference for the History of Education*, vol. 2, ed. Sándor Komlósi(Pécs: Janus Pannonius University, 1987), 102.

3 John Dewey, "The Development of American Pragmatism," in *The Later Works of John Dewey. The Electronic Edition. Volume 2: 1925–1927* (Charlottesville, VA: Intelex Corporation 1925), 19.

4 Throughout his extensive pedagogical work, the Jesuit priest Ramón
Ruiz Amado makes no mention of John Dewey, a name that to him
only evoked the battle of Cavite [Antonio Sangüesa, *Pedagogía y
Clericismo en la Obra del P. Ramón Ruiz Amado* (Zurich: PAS 1973),
153 note 43]. Another leading Catholic pedagogue of the time,
Rufino Blanco y Rubio, seems to have been more familiar with
Dewey, who he cites several times in the second edition of his *Teoría
de la Educación*, especially regarding manual work and social cooperation. Overall, they are aseptic references mixed with those of other
authors, and do not enter into the main point of Deweyan philosophy. Rufino Blanco identifies Dewey more with the sociological
approach and authors such as Natorp and Foester than with the
pragmatism of James [Blanco y Rufino Sánchez, *Teoría de la Educación*, vol. 1 (Madrid: Librería y Casa Editorial Hernando 1930),
43].

5 See, for example, G.J.J. Biesta and S. Miedema, "Dewey in Europe: A
Case Study on the International Dimensions of the Turn-of-the-
Century Educational Reform," *American Journal of Education* 105
(1996): 1–26; G.J.J. Biesta and S. Miedema, Context and Interaction.
How to Assess Dewey's Influence on Educational Reform in Europe?
Studies in Philosophy and Education 19, nos 1–2 (2000): 21–37;
Thomas S. Popkewitz, ed. *Inventing the Modern Self and John
Dewey: Modernities and the Traveling of Pragmatism in Education*
(New York: Palgrave Macmillan, 2005).

6 Antonio Viñao, *Escuela para Todos. Educación y Modernidad en la
España del Siglo XX.* (Madrid: Marcial Pons Historia, 2004), 27.

7 Antonio Jiménez García, *El Krausismo y la Institución Libre de
Enseñanza* (Madrid: Cincel, 1985); Enrique M. Ureña, *El Krausismo
Alemán. Los Congresos de Filósofos y el Krausofröbelismo* (Madrid:
Universidad Pontificia Comillas, 2002).

8 Francisco Giner de los Ríos, "El Problema de la Educación Popular y
las Clases 'Productoras'," in *Educación y Enseñanza* (Madrid: La
Lectura, 1900/1925), 231.

9 Joaquín Xirau, "Julián Sanz del Río y el Krausismo Español,"

Cuadernos Americanos 16 (1944): 62, quoted in Elias Díaz, *La Filosofía Social del Krausismo* (Madrid: Edicusa, 1973), 51–2.

10 Díaz, *La Filosofía Social del Krausismo,* 17ff.

11 Solomon Lipp, *Francisco Giner de los Rios: A Spanish Socrates* (Waterloo, ON: Wilfrid Laurier University Press, 1985), 9.

12 Letter from Röder to Giner de los Ríos (Heidelberg, 30 March 1870) in *Giner de los Ríos y los Krausistas Alemanes. Correspondencia inédita, eds.* Enrique M. Ureña and José M. Vázquez-Romero (Madrid: Universidad Complutense, 2003), 38.

13 Letter from Leonhardi to Giner de los Ríos (Prague, 21 March 1872) in ibid., 65–70. "Old-Catholics" designates those who rejected the dogma of Papal infallibility, proclaimed at the Vatican I Council, as an innovation contrary to the traditional faith of the Church.

14 Letter from Giner to Leonhardi (n.d., probably 1873), in ibid., 89.

15 Paul Misner, "Catholic Anti-Modernism: The Ecclesial Settings," in *Catholicism Contending with Modernity. Roman Catholic Modernism and Anti-Modernism in Historical Context,* ed. Darrell Jodock (Cambridge: Cambridge University Press, 2000), 64.

16 The same year the Council finished, Leonhardi published the article "Sätze zu einer Vergleichen den Betrachtung des Glaubens und des Wissens, der Wissenschaft und der Religion. Ein Beitrag zur Verständigung" (Propositions for a Comparative Consideration of Faith and Knowledge, Science and Religion: An Article for Understanding) in the journal *Die Neue Zeit,* no. II (Prague 1870). In it, he maintained the compatibility of scientific, rational knowledge and religious faith, and from there, the error in defending dogmas: "The attempt at ensuring the propagation of divine individual revelation in a tutelary way by shutting it into formulas of Faith (so-called dogmas), externally obligated, taken away from free examination, could only be successful – and even then only dubiously and blindly – in times before reaching spiritual adulthood; but once adulthood arrives, such an attempt would hurt more than it gained, being the suppression of that coercive form of Faith, a worthy need in the well-understood interest of Religion" (Hermann Karl von Leonhardi, "Religión y

Ciencia. Bases para Determinar sus Relaciones," in *Estudios Filosóficos y Religiosos,* ed. Francisco Giner de los Ríos, [Madrid: Librería de Francisco Góngora, 1870/1876], 286–7). This work was translated and published by Giner de los Ríos upon Leonhardi's death in 1876 in his book *Estudios Filosóficos y Religiosos [Studies on Philosophy and Religion]*, along with other articles that reflect the preeminence of the religious problem at the time. In one of these articles, also from 1876, Giner de los Ríos examines the stance of the Old Catholics, who did not accept the dogma of papal infallibility and held principles nearer those of the Protestant confessions. He distinguished three general trends in terms of the religious positions of the time: the dogmatic, represented by the stance of the church; the atheist, the most common whether declared openly or not; and the rationalist, based on natural religion. Giner de los Ríos distrusted the ability of any of these three ways to solve the conflict between natural religion and revealed religion, a sign of which was the schism produced in the heart of the Catholic Church. In his opinion, such a solution had better chances of occurring "by a gradual transformation of the sense, doctrine, practices, and organizations of the Christian communions." Francisco Giner de los Ríos, "Los Católicos Viejos y el Espíritu Contemporáneo," in ibid., 349.

17 José Luís Abellán, *Historia Crítica del Pensamiento Español,* Vol. IV (Madrid: Espasa-Calpe, 1984), 455.

18 Díaz, *La Filosofía Social del Krausismo,* 22–3.

19 Giner de los Ríos, Prologue, in *Educación y Enseñanza,* (1889/1925), 5.

20 Francisco Giner de los Ríos, "La Educación Moral en la Escuela Según Mr. G.G. Myers," in *Ensayos Menores sobre Educación y Enseñanza. Tomo I.* (Madrid: La Lectura 1908/1927), 243; and Francisco Giner de los Ríos, "La Política y la Escuela Según Kelsen," in ibid., 260–1, note 2.

21 Eugenio Otero Urtaza, "La Irrupción de la Pedagogía en la Universidad Española: Manuel Bartolomé Cossío en la Cátedra de Pedagogía Superior," *Revista de Educación* 332(2003):256–7.

22 Manuel Bartolomé Cossío, "La Enseñanza en los Estados Unidos y su

Organización," *Boletín de la Institución Libre de Enseñanza* 13, no. 307(1889): 337–9; Manuel Bartolomé Cossío, "Notas sobre Inspección Escolar en los Estados Unidos," *Boletín de la Institución Libre de Enseñanza* 14 No. 323 (1890): 212–15.

23 Institución Libre de Enseñanza, "El Movimiento de las Ideas Pedagógicas en los Estados Unidos," *Boletín de la Institución Libre de Enseñanza* 33, no. 462 (1898): 271–6.

24 In fact, this text is largely unknown and the first Spanish translation of *My Pedagogic Creed* is still considered to be the one published in Chile in 1908 by Darío E. Sálas. Cfr. Antón Donoso, "John Dewey in Spain and in Spanish America," *International Philosophical Quarterly* 41, no 3 (2001): 349.

25 Urtaza, "La Irrupción de la Pedagogía en la Universidad Española," 254–7.

26 Jay Martin, *The Education of John Dewey: A Biography* (New York: Columbia University Press, 2000), 210–31.

27 Manuel Bartolomé Cossío, "El maestro, la escuela y el material de enseñanza" (Madrid: La lectura n.d.): 21 (Conference presented in Bilbao in 1905). "Learning by Doing," in English in the original text.

28 As in Madrid, Dewey's ideas in Catalonia were welcomed by a core of people involved in movements for pedagogic modernization, mainly Eladi Homs and Joan Palau. Homs went to the United States from 1907 to 1910 for independent study at the University of Chicago's School of Education. In America, he became aware of the ideas of James and Dewey and made them known through his collaborations in several Catalonian periodicals. (Vid. Eladi Homs, *Articles pedagògics*, Vic, Eumo Editorial [2002].) Joan Palau, founder of the school *Collegi Mont d'Or* and disseminator of the pedagogy of Maria Montessori, translated *My Pedagogic Creed* into Catalan, and it was published 1917 and 1918 in *Quaderns D'Estudi*, a journal dependent on the Council on Pedagogic Research of the Barcelona Regional Government and promoted by Homs and Eugeni D'Ors (John Dewey, El Meu Credo Pedagògic, *Quaderns d'Estudi* 1, nos 2 and 4 [1917–18], 129–34 and 252–9, translated by Joan Palau Vera).

29 Richard Rorty, "A World without Substances or Essences," *Philosophy and Social Hope* (London: Penguin Books, 1994/1999), 52.

30 Based on León Esteban Mateo, *Boletín de la Institución Libre de Enseñanza. Nómina bibliográfica (1877–1976)*(Valencia: Universidad de Valencia, 1978).

31 For Spanish authors, there are only two articles from Barnés, one dedicated to "The Pedagogy of Pragmatism" (Domingo Barnés, "La pedagogía del pragmatism," *Boletín de la Institución Libre de Enseñanza* 45, no. 732 [1921]: 72–4), and the other to "The Pedagogy of John Dewey" (Domingo Barnés "La pedagogía de John Dewey," *Boletín de la Institución Libre de Enseñanza* 50 no. 797 [1926]: 238–47), which is his introduction to the collected works of Dewey, *La escuela y el niño* (*School and the Child*).

32 John Dewey, "La escuela y el progreso social," *Boletín de la Institución Libre de Enseñanza* 39, nos 662-33 (1915):129–34 and 161–5.

33 Eugeni D'Ors, Comment on the book of Emile Boutroux, *William James, Arxius de l'Institut de Ciencies* I/1, (1911), 151–2. Reprinted in Eugeni D'Ors, *La Filosofía del Hombre que Trabaja y que Juega* (Madrid: Libertarias/Prodhufi, 1995), 116–21.

34 Émile Boutroux, *William James* (Paris: A. Colin, 1911), 137–42.

35 Émile Boutroux, "La pedagogía de William James," *Boletín de la Institución Libre de Enseñanza* 35, no. 617 (1911): 228–31.

36 Boutroux, *William James*, 128.

37 Daniel Tröhler, "Langue as Homeland: The Genevan Reception of Dewey in the Challenge of Modernity," in *Inventing the Modern Self and John Dewey*, ed. T. Popkewitz, (Palgrave Macmillan 2005), 68.

38 Edouard Claparède, "La Pedagogía de J. Dewey," *Boletín de la Institución Libre de Enseñanza* 46, no. 753 (1922): 353–61.

39 Tröhler, "Langue as Homeland," 69. On the evolution of the focus of attention in the European new education movement from the individual's to society's needs, see for instance, Kevin J. Brehony, "A New Education for a New Era: The Contribution of the Conferences of the New Education Fellowship to the Disciplinary Field of Education 1921–1938," *Paedagogica Historica* 40, nos 5 and 6 (2004): 733–55.

40 Edouard Claparède, "La Pédagogie de M. John Dewey," in John

Dewey, *L'École et l'Enfant,* 3rd ed. (Neuchatel/Paris: Delachaux et Niestlé, 1913/1931), 8, note 1. Claparède refers to the article Dewey published in 1908 on James's *Pragmatism, a New Name for Some Old Ways of Thinking.* (John Dewey, "What Does Pragmatism Mean by Practical?" *The Journal of Philosophy, Psychology and Scientific Methods* 5 [1908]: 85–99.) In *L'éducation fonctionelle,* Claparéde takes a different view, and states that Dewey's instrumentalism "is nothing more than a variety of pragmatism." Edouard Claparède, *L'éducation fonctionelle* (Neuchâtel/Paris: Delachaux et Niestlé 1931/1968), 25.

41 At the Third International Congress for Philosophy that took place at the University of Heidelberg in September 1908, Störring acknowledged the importance of pragmatism "for the question of the psychogenesis of thought, but not in a logical-epistemological context" (quoted in Jürgen Oelkers, "Remarks on the Conceptualization of John Dewey's Democracy and Education," Lecture for the Annual John Dewey Society Symposium April 11, 2005 AERA Meeting in Montreal [2005]: 2.) Shortly before (in his lectures in Boston and New York in 1906 and 1907) James himself had mockingly commented tongue-in-cheek on the attempt to lower the true concept of pragmatism to one that could be valid for psychology but not for philosophy: "Pragmatism is uncomfortable away from facts. Rationalism is comfortable only in the presence of abstractions. This pragmatist talk about truths in the plural, about their utility and satisfactions, about the success with which they 'work', etc., suggests to the typical intellectualist mind a sort of coarse lame second-rate makeshift article of truth. Such truths are not real truth. Such tests are merely subjective. As against this, objective truth must be something non-utilitarian, haughty, refined, remote, august, exalted. It must be an absolute correspondence of our thoughts with an equally absolute reality. It must be what we ought to think unconditionally. The conditioned ways in which we do think are so much irrelevance and matter for psychology. Down with psychology, up with logic, in all this question!" (William James, *Pragmatism, a New Name for some Old Ways of Thinking. Popular Lec-*

tures on Philosophy [New York: Longmans, Green, and Co., 1908], 67.)

42 Claparède, "La pédagogie de M. John Dewey," 13–14.

43 Rosa M. Cardá and Helio Carpintero, *Domingo Barnés: Psicología y educación* (Alicante: Instituto de Cultura Juan Gil-Albert, 1993), 38.

44 Edouard Claparède, "La Psicología de las Aptitudes," *Revista de Pedagogía* II, no. 18 (1923): 223–7. Claparède had also traveled to Catalonia three years previously to give a course at the Escola d'Estiu in Barcelona.

45 Cardá and Carpintero, *Domingo Barnés*, 92.

46 Ibid., 163.

47 Ibid., 88 and 92.

48 William James, *Principios de Psicología*. (Madrid: Daniel Jorro, 1900).

49 Barnés, "La Pedagogía del Pragmatismo," 72–4.

50 John Dewey, *La escuela y la sociedad* (Madrid: Francisco Beltrán, n.d.). The translation is from one of the reprints of the book, in 1900, which presents three lectures delivered by Dewey at the University Elementary School in April 1899, plus an additional text from a talk by Dewey at a meeting of the Parents' Association of the school in February of that same year. For some time, it was maintained that the Spanish publication of *School and Society*, allegedly in 1900, was the first book by Dewey to be published in another language. This assumption was based on a reference in the Dewey *Checklist of Translations* (Jo Ann Boydson, *John Dewey: A Checklist of Translations, 1900–1967* [Carbondale: Southern Illinois University Press, 1969], 49). This assumption is now known to be incorrect, and though there is still some doubt about the exact date of the original publication of the Spanish translation, it is reasonable to place it between 1915 and 1918 (Jaime Nubiola and Beatriz Sierra, "La Recepción de Dewey en España y Latinoamérica," *Utopía y Praxis Latinoamericana* 6, no. 13 [2001]: 107–19; Jaime Nubiola, "The Reception of Dewey in the Hispanic World," *Studies in Philosophy and Education* 24, no. 6 [2005]: 437–53.) The text Barnés uses as a prologue coincides with a comment to Dewey's book, published by

the Spanish author in his 1917 book *Fuentes para el estudio de la paidología* (Domingo Barnés, *Fuentes para el estudio de la paidología* [Madrid: Imp. de la Revista de Arch., Bibl. y Museos, 1917], 193–200). In this book, Dewey carries far less weight than that given to Stanley Hall.

51 Barnés, Prologue, in John Dewey, *La escuela y la sociedad*, 7.

52 Ibid., 6.

53 John Dewey, "L'école et le progrès social," *L'Éducation* 1 (1909): 198–217.

54 John Dewey, *La escuela y el niño* (Madrid: La Lectura, 1926), 7–36. Barnés's prologue was also published that year in the *Boletín de la Institución Libre de Enseñanza*. Domingo Barnés, "La Pedagogía de J. Dewey," *Boletín de la Institución Libre de Enseñanza* 50, no. 797 (1926): 238–47.

55 J.J. Findlay, *The School and the Child. Being Selections from the Educational Essays of John Dewey* (London: Blachie and Son, n.d.).

56 Barnés, Prólogo, in John Dewey, *La escuela y el niño*, 14.

57 "Dewey repeatedly states that 'personality and character are more important than the study matter.' The purpose is neither knowledge nor information, but self-fulfillment." Barnés, Prólogo, 16.

58 Ibid., 16.

59 Ibid., 25.

60 Oelkers, "Remarks on the Conceptualization of John Dewey's Democracy and Education," 9.

61 John Dewey, (1916) *Democracy and Education*, in *The Middle Works of John Dewey. The Electronic Edition. Volume 9: 1916.* (Charlottesville, VA: Intelex Corporation), 63.

62 Barnés, Prólogo, 25.

63 Ibid., 31.

64 John Dewey, "Democracy and Education," in *Cyclopedia of Education* vol. II, ed. Paul Monroe(New York: Macmillan Co., 1911), 293.

65 Ibid.

66 James Scott Johnston, *Inquiry and Education: John Dewey and the Quest for Democracy* (Albany, NY: State University of New York Press, 2006), 156.

67 In 1918 the *Boletín de la Institución Libre de Enseñanza* had published the translation of a review by A. Kohler on Dewey's book. A. Kohler, "La Democracia y la Educación de John Dewey," *Boletín de la Institución Libre de Enseñanza* 42 no. 699 (1918): 161–2.

68 Volumes 3, 4, and 5 of the complete works published in the collection "Ciencia y Educación Contemporanea" (*Science and Contemporáry Education*) The complete collection includes: 1. *La escuela y el niño* (*School and the Child*, foreword by D. Barnés) (1926); 2. *Ensayos de educación* (*Essays on Education*) (1926); 3. *Teorías sobre la educación: Democracia y educación* (*Theories on Education: Democracy and Education*) (1926); 4. *Los fines, las materias y los métodos de la educación: La educación y la democracia. II* (*The Aims, Matters and Methods of Education: Education and Democracy II*) (1927); 5. *Filosofía de la educación. Los valores educativos: Educación y democracia. III* (*Philosophy of Education. Values in Education: Education and Democracy III*) (1927), 6. *Cómo pensamos* (*How We Think*) (1928); 7. *El hábito y el impulso en la conducta* (*Habit and Impulse in Behavior*) (1929); and 8. *La inteligencia y la conducta* (*Intelligence and Behavior*) (1930). The same publisher also printed *Reconstrucción de la filosofía* (*Reconstruction of Philosophy*) (1930). Chapter 7 of *Democracy and Education* had been published previously in 1925 in the *Boletín*. John Dewey, "La Concepción Democrática de la Educación," *Boletín de la Institución Libre de Enseñanza* 49, nos 788/789 (1925): 327–8/353–8.

69 Herminio Barreiro, *Lorenzo Luzuriaga y la Renovación Educativa en España (1889–1936)* (A Coruña: Edición Do Castro, 1989), 118.

70 Ibid.

71 Lorenzo Luzuriaga, "La Pedagogía de Dewey. La Educación por la Acción," *El Sol* (22 April 1918): 8.

72 Barreiro, *Lorenzo Luzuriaga y la Renovación Educativa en España (1889–1936)*, 101–32. Alejando Tiana, "Educación, Cultura y Clase Obrera," *Homenaje a Pablo Iglesias* (Madrid: Escuela Julián-Besteiro, Decembre 2000): 8–9 (unpublished paper).

73 Luzuriaga, *La pedagogía de Dewey. La educación por la acción*, 8.

74 Ibid.

75 John Dewey and Evelyn Dewey, *Las escuelas de mañana* (Madrid: Lib. de los Sucesores de Hernando, 1918).

76 John Dewey and Evelyn Dewey, "Industria y Organización Educativa," *Boletín de la Institución Libre de Enseñanza* 42, no. 698 (1918):100–7.

77 Lorenzo Luzuriaga, "La pedagogía de John Dewey," in John Dewey, *El niño y el programa escolar.* (Madrid: Publicaciones de la Revista de Pedagogía, 1925): 7.

78 By 1925, there were at least three editions of the Creed in Spain: one from *Boletín de la Institución Libre de Enseñanza*, from 1898, a Catalan edition from 1917–18, and an abridged edition also published in the *Boletín* in 1924 (John Dewey, "Mi Credo Pedagógico," *Boletín de la Institución Libre de Enseñanza* 48, no. 776 (1924): 330–1). Many others would join the list in the following years.

79 Barreiro, *Lorenzo Luzuriaga y la Renovación Educativa en España,* 160–92.

80 Luzuriaga, "La pedagogía de John Dewey," 14.

81 In one of these works on the notion of *Arbeitschule*, written in Berlin in 1914, Luzuriaga says John Dewey and American pedagogy are the most characteristic representatives of the impulse given to the principle of activity by the adaptation to the needs of daily life. He further adds that examples of this principle "are found in the organization of the schools in Munich by Kerschensteiner and in the schools in Chicago and Rome directed by John Dewey and Maria Montessori, respectively," revealing that he still had some trouble placing the American philosopher at that time. Lorenzo Luzuriaga, "La Escuela del Trabajo," *La Inspección de Primera Enseñanza* 1, no. 3 (1914): 13.

82 Lorenzo Luzuriaga, "La Pedagogía de Kerschensteiner," *Boletín de la Institución Libre de Enseñanza* 42, no. 701 (1918): 238.

83 Ibid.

84 Jorge Kerschensteiner, "La Escuela del Trabajo," *Revista de Pedagogía* 1, no. 9 (1922): 321–9. In 1926, the *Revista de Pedagogía* published a second work by Kerschensteiner, Jorge Kerschensteiner, "El Autogobierno de los Alumnos," *Revista de Pedagogía* 5, no. 49 (1926): 18–24.

85 Jorge Kerschensteiner, *Concepto de la Escuela del Trabajo* (Madrid:
    La Lectura, n.d., probably 1923); Jorge Kerschensteiner, *El Problema
    de la Educación Pública* (Madrid: Publicaciones de la Revista de Ped-
    agogía, 1925).

86 Lorenzo Luzuriaga, "La pedagogía de Jorge Kerschensteiner," in *El
    Problema de la Educación Pública,* ed. Jorge Kerschensteiner
    (Madrid: Publicaciones de la Revista de Pedagogía, 1925): 6. This
    study was also partially published in Lorenzo Luzuriaga, "La Peda-
    gogía de Jorge Kerschensteiner," *Revista de Pedagogía* 4, no. 42
    (1925): 249–50.

87 Jorge Kerschensteiner, "The School of the Future a School of Manual
    Work," in *The Schools and the Nation* (London: MacMillan and
    Co., 1908/1914), 128, footnote.

88 Philipp Gonon, "Education, not Democracy? The Apolitical Dewey,"
    Studies in Philosophy and Education 19, nos. 1–2 (2000): 141–57.
    Regarding this correspondence, Bittner writes: "In some letters from
    1914 Spranger urges the town school-inspector to reconsider his
    praise of Dewey from the year 1908. It is not probable that Spranger
    did not react to Kerschensteiner's first Dewey emphasis until six years
    later. From references to previous letters we can assume that the first
    and – with regard to the German Dewey adoption – probably most
    interesting part of Spranger's writings to Kerschensteiner has been
    lost. Kerschensteiner then holds back with his public acknowledge-
    ment of Dewey's instrumentalism until the beginning of the Weimar-
    era. Alwin Papst and other enthusiastic Dewey followers were sum-
    moned before the main committee of the "Verein für
    wissenschaftliche Bildung" where they were dissuaded from support-
    ing the decisive positions of the American pedagogue. The now-
    changed opinions were published as 'minutes'." S. Bittner, German
    Readers of Dewey – Before 1933 and After 1945," *Studies in Philos-
    ophy and Education* 19, nos. 1–2 (2000): 83–108.

89 Barreiro, *Lorenzo Luzuriaga y la Renovación Educativa en España
    (1889–1936),* 259.

90 John Dewey, "La Educación y los Problemas Sociales Actuales,"
    *Revista de Pedagogía*12, no. 140 (1933): 327–44.

91 John Dewey, "El Futuro del Liberalismo," *Revista de Pedagogía* 14, no. 157 (1935):126–31.

92 Lorenzo Luzuriaga, "La Escuela en Unidad," *La Inspección de Primera Enseñanza* 1, no. 1 (1914): 6–7. Lorenzo Luzuriaga was not the first to have reported in Spain about the "unique school," which others had described earlier. For instance María de Maeztu referred to this idea in 1910 during a trip to Europe. Teresa Marín, *Innovadores de la educación en España* (Cuenca: Universidad de Castilla-La Mancha, 1991), 211.

93 Lorenzo Luzuriaga, "La Escuela del Trabajo," 11.

94 Lorenzo Luzuriaga, *La escuela única* (Madrid: Publicaciones de la Revista de Pedagogía, 1931), 22–3.

95 The unique school, says Luzuriaga, strives to be "a school for everyone, for the religious and the atheists, for the rich and the poor; where the son of a government minister, for example, sits next to the son of a worker as they do in Bavaria or Switzerland; in short, a school that is not the school of castes. And most of all, a school not belonging to the township or the church, but to the civil community, to the nation, to the State, charged with informing the national spirit." Lorenzo Luzuriaga, "La escuela en unidad," 7.

96 Cfr. John Dewey, *The School and Society*, in *The Middle Works of John Dewey. The Electronic Edition. Volume 1: 1899–1901* (Charlottesville, VA: Intelex Corporation, 1899), 64.

97 See, for example, John Dewey, "Liberal Education," in *A Cyclopedia of Education,* vol. 4, ed. Paul Monroe (New York: Macmillan, 1913), 4–6. Luzuriaga perceives this unity from the point of view of the work school, (Luzuriaga, "La Escuela del Trabajo," 15). However, when shaping an education proposal on school organization, he goes back to separating the two types of education, as he did in his report for the Spanish Workers' Socialist Party program in 1918. In the report, the aim of giving form to the unique school does not impede the existence of separate institutions for general education and professional education. La Escuela Nueva "Bases para un Programa de Instrucción Pública," *Boletín de la Institución Libre de Enseñanza* 42, no. 705 (1918): 361.

98 This copy remains among the books from Dewey's library, with a dedication by Lorenzo Luzuriaga dated 15 May 1946. (Cfr. *The Correspondence of John Dewey, 1871–1952*. Electronic edition. Note to the letter 09852 [1942.08.28]. Checked at the Center for Dewey Studies, Carbondale, IL on 26 July 2006).

99 Lorenzo Luzuriaga, *Historia de la Educación Pública* (Buenos Aires: Losada, 1946/1964), 135.

100 Ibid., 147.

101 Ibid., 151.

102 Dewey, *Democracy and Education*, 104.

103 Ibid., 116.

104 Evelina Orteza y Miranda, "Pragmatism and the Child: John Dewey," in *Studies in Childhood History. A Canadian Perspective*, eds. Patricia T. Rooke and R.L. Schnell (Calgary: Detselig Enterprises Limited, 1982): 29–56.

105 Dewey, *Democracy and Education*, 93.

106 Ibid., 82.

107 Ibid, 104.

108 Barreiro, *Lorenzo Luzuriaga y la Renovación Educativa en España (1889–1936)*, 157–8.

109 José Ortega y Gasset, "Prólogo para Franceses," in *La Rebelión de las Masas* (Madrid: Círculo de Lectores, 1937/1967): 38. Ortega y Gasset had written on this idea in a comment from 1928 on Hegel's *Philosophy of Universal History*. José Ortega y Gasset, "Hegel y América," in *El Espectador. Tomos VII y VIII* (Madrid: Espasa-Calpe, 1928/1966): 11–27.

110 José Ortega y Gasset, "Medio Siglo de Filosofía," *Revista de Occidente* 3 (1951/1980): 15.

111 Ibid., 14.

112 Ortega y Gasset's relationship with pragmatism has been treated in the doctoral dissertation by Eduardo J. Armenteros, *El pragmatismo de Ortega. Una "Impronta" de su filosofía*. Universidad de Sevilla (2004). ·

113 José Ortega y Gasset, "Pedagogía y Anacronismo," in *Misión de la*

Universidad y otros Ensayos sobre Educación y Pedagogía (Madrid: Revista de Occidente, 1923/1982), 155–8.

114 *The Correspondence of John Dewey, 1871–1952.* Electronic edition. Letter 03152 (1925.06.28), Elizabeth Braley Dewey to Dewey family. Checked at the Center for Dewey Studies, Carbondale, Illinois, on 26 July 2006. Dykhuizen, following Schack, places this trip in summer 1926. George Dykhuizen, *The Life and Mind of John Dewey* (Carbondale and Edwardsville: Southern Illinois University Press, 1973), 222–3; W. Schack, *Art and Argyrol. The Life and Career of Dr. Albert C. Barnes* (New York: A.S. Barnes and Company, 1963), 191.

115 John Dewey, "Aid for the Spanish Government," *Christian Century,* (3 March 1937): 202.

116 University Federation for Democracy and Intellectual Freedom – *An Open Letter On Culture and Democracy in Spain* (New York: University Federation for Democracy and Intellectual Freedom, 1938).

117 Eugeni D'Ors, "Dewey i Fichte," *Quaderns d'Estudi* 2, no. 1 (1917): 88–95.

118 John Dewey, "Froebel's Educational Principles," in *The Middle Works of John Dewey. The electronic edition. Volume 1: 1899–1901* (Charlottesville, VA: Intelex Corporation, 1900): 81–91.

119 Dewey, *Democracy and Education,* 61.

120 Jaime Nubiola and Izaskun Martínez, "The Reception of William James in Spain and Unamuno's Reading of 'Varieties'," *Streams of William James* 5, no. 2 (2003): 7–9; Marta Torregrosa, "El pragmatismo en el pensamiento de Eugenio d'Ors," *Anuario Filosófico* 40, no. 2 (2007): 373–87.

121 Letter from D'Ors to Giner (Paris, June 3, 1909), in Vicente Cacho Viu, *Revisión de Eugenio D'Ors (1902–1930), Seguida de un Epistolario Inédito* (Barcelona: Quaderns Crema, 1977), 198–99.

122 Published in Th. Elsenhans, ed., *Bericht über den III. Internationalen Kongress für Philosophie zu Heidelberg 1. bis 5. September 1908* (Heidelberg: Carl Winter 1909). Spanish editions: Eugeni D'Ors, "El Residuo en la Medida de la Ciencia por la Acción," *Boletín de la Institución Libre de Enseñanza* 33, no. 591 (1909): 187–91; and

Eugeni D'Ors, *Religio est Libertas* (Madrid: Imp. Ciudad Lineal, 1925). Partially reprinted in D'Ors, *La Filosofía del Hombre que Trabaja y que Juega.*

123 George Stuart Fullerton, "The Meeting of the Third International Congress of Philosophy, at Heidelberg, August 31 to September 5, 1908," *The Journal of Philosophy, Psychology and Scientific Methods* 5, no. 21 (1908): 573–7.

124 Enrique Tierno Galván, *Idealismo y Pragmatismo en el s. XIX Español* (Madrid: Tecnos, 1977).

125 Juan López-Morillas, *Racionalismo pragmático. El pensamiento de Francisco Giner de los Ríos* (Madrid: Alianza, 1988).

126 In reference to the "harmonious rationalism" of Krause.

127 Letter from D'Ors to Giner, 200.

128 Albert Schinz, *Anti-Pragmatisme: Examen des Droits Respectifs de l'Aristocratie Intellectuelle et de la Democratie Sociale* (Paris: Félix Alcan, 1909).

129 William James, *Pragmatism, a New Name for Some Old Ways of Thinking; Popular Lectures on Philosophy* (New York: Longmans, Green, and Co., 1908), 20. Vid. Pedro Cerezo Galán, *El Mal del Siglo: El Conflicto entre Ilustración y Romanticismo en la Crisis Finisecular del Siglo XX* (Madrid: Alianza, 2003), 41–61.

130 Nicolás Salmerón, "Prólogo," in *Filosofía y Arte* Hermenegildo Giner, (Madrid: Imprenta de M. Minuesa, 1878): XIII.

131 John L. Childs, *American Pragmatism and Education* (New York: Henry Holt and Company, 1956), 315–21.

132 John Dewey, *Religion and Our Schools*, in *The Middle Works of John Dewey. The Electronic Edition. Volume 4: 1907–1909* (Charlottesville, VA: Intelex Corporation, 1908), 176–77.

133 In 1877 the Institution made both Charles Darwin and the Belgian Krausist Guillaume Tiberghien honorary professors. Institución Libre de Enseñanza Noticias, *Boletín de la Institución Libre de Enseñanza* I, no. 21 (1877): 123. On the weight of Darwinism and Hegelianism in Dewey's philosophy, see, for instance: James T. Kloppenberg *Uncertain Victory: Social Democracy and Progressivism in European and American Thought, 1870–1920* (New York: Oxford University

Press, 1986); Richard Rorty, "Dewey between Hegel and Darwin," in *Rorty and Pragmatism,* ed. Herman J. Saatkamp (Nashville and London: Vanderbilt University Press, 1995), 1–15; Victor Kestenbaum, *The Grace and the Severity of the Ideal. John Dewey and the Transcendent* (Chicago: Chicago University Press, 2002).

134 James, *Pragmatism,* 33 and 284.

135 F. Giner de los Ríos, "La ciencia como función social," in *Filosofia y Sociologia* (Barcelona: Imprenta de Henrich y Ca., 1897/1904): 16, note. The text comes from a work sent by Giner to be read at the Third Congress of the International Institute of Sociology held in Paris in July 1897, at which great discussion was made of the organic theory of society. R. Worms, Miscellany: Third Congress of the International Institute of Sociology, held at Paris, July 21–24, 1897. *The Annals of the American Academy of Political and Social Science* 11(1898): 109–12.

136 James, *Pragmatism,* 70.

137   Ibid., 17 and 18.

138 "A remote goal of complete unfoldedness is, in technical philosophic language, transcendental. That is, it is something apart from direct experience and perception." Dewey, *Democracy and Education, 63.*

139 J. Gaos, Prólogo del Traductor, in John Dewey, *La Experiencia y la Naturaleza* (México: F.C.E., 1948): xix–xxx.

140 Domingo Barnés, "Un Aspecto de la Filosofía de los Valores y la Pedagogía," in *Ensayos de Pedagogía y Filosofía* (Madrid: La Lectura, 1920/n.d.): 43.

141 Ibid., 45.

142 Ibid.

143 James, *Pragmatism,* 72.

144 Ibid., 74.

145 *The Correspondence of John Dewey, 1871–1952.* Electronic edition. Letter: 09852 (1942.08.28), Lorenzo Luzuriaga to John Dewey. Checked at the Center for Dewey Studies, Carbondale, IL, on 26 July 2006.

146 I.L. Kandel, "The Influence of John Dewey Abroad," *School and Society* 30, no. 778 (1929): 702.

147 John Dewey, "Experience and Education," in *The Later Works of John Dewey. The Electronic Edition. Volume 13: 1938–1939* (Charlottesville, VA: Intelex Corporation, 1938), 14. *Experience and Education* was also translated into Spanish by Luzuriaga, in exile. John Dewey, *Experiencia y Educación* (Buenos Aires: Losada, 1939).

148 John Dewey, "The Influence of Darwinism on Philosophy," in *The Middle Works of John Dewey. The electronic edition. Volume 4: 1907–1909* (Charlottesville,VA: Intelex Corporation, 1909), 19.

149 Norbert Elias, *El Proceso de la Civilización. Investigaciones Psicogénicas y Sociogénicas* (México: Fondo de Cultura Económica, 1939/1993), 449–63.

150 Ortega y Gasset, "Medio Siglo de Filosofía," 17.

4

To those in "Heathen Darkness"
Deweyan Democracy and Education in the American Interdenominational Configuration – the Case of the Committee on Cooperation in Latin America

ROSA BRUNO-JOFRÉ

INTRODUCTION:
CONFIGURING THE MISSIONARY GOALS

Protestants in the United States began to pay increasing attention to the cause of foreign missions as early as the nineteenth century. By the beginning of the twentieth century there were some ninety missionary societies at work as well as various global associations. In the 1880s, the debates around Christianization and civilization and the impact of modernism on mainline Protestantism had gradually changed into a broader political discussion that took place within the context of the social gospel and various progressive movements. The social gospel sought to apply the Christian message of salvation to society as well as to the individual in an urban, industrial age.[1] It was preoccupied with the socialized individual and the Christianization of society. The goal of building the kingdom of God on earth (which was later translated by social gospel educators into the democracy of God) gained a place in missionary work. Along the way, the missionaries created spaces of interaction and potential influence that were framed by configurations of ideas, including a spiritualized notion of John Dewey's understanding of democracy and education, and reference horizons provided by particular socio-cultural settings.[2]

The Ecumenical Conference on Foreign Missions, the first conference in North America that could legitimately be called ecumenical, was apologetic in character and took place in 1900 in New York City, attracting 1,700 delegates and 600 foreign missionaries.[3] In 1910 the World Missionary Conference took place in Edinburgh and was seen as marking an organizational advance because its approach and preparation furthered "a new science of missions on the field," meaning that the conference had a representative character (based on the selection of delegates), the participants had done research on the issues, and the conference exhibited "deliberative efficiency." It was a time of disciplinary emergence, professionalization of the sciences, and the development of transnational forms of knowledge. The Edinburgh Conference did not include representatives from Latin America because it did not deal with countries that were, at least nominally, Catholic; however, informal meetings of delegates whose work was in Latin America led to the creation of a committee that wrote a statement to be presented to North American churches. The statement said, among other things, "The Church must not forget that missions in the Latin and Oriental Christian countries are and have long been a legitimate part of the foreign missionary enterprise of the leading foreign missionary Societies of the United States and Canada. As such they could claim the right to consideration in any World Missionary Conference."[4] Two years later the Foreign Missions Conference of North America made arrangements for a conference on Latin America, which took place in New York City in March 1913. At that conference a committee to deal with Latin America and the issue of cooperation – the Committee on Cooperation in Latin America – was created. Its first move was to contact missionaries in each Latin American country and arrange preparatory meetings for organizing a conference in Latin America.[5] The leaders involved in the Committee and in the preparation of the first Latin American conference, which would come to be known as Panama Congress 1916, were influential in the ecumenical and international movement: Dr Robert E. Speer, who called for "the evangelization of the world in this generation," was appointed chairperson of the Committee; Rev. Samuel G. Inman, a political voice of the Social Gospel in Latin America and of Pan-Americanism, was appointed secretary; and John Mott, who led the Student Volunteer Movement of Foreign Missions (organized in 1888), was in charge of organizing the conference. Another interesting member of the Committee was Rev. Josiah Strong, who believed that the traditions of Protestantism and social and political liberalism advocated by the Anglo-Saxons would dominate the future.[6] The creation of the Committee was in line with the increasing influence of the social gospel and the interdenominational efforts that had become an important aim of Protestantism in America. It is relevant to note here that in 1908 the Federal Council of Churches of Christ in America had produced the Social Creed of the Churches, a statement of social ethics that, as Rossinow said, defined the domestic policies of the Council for a generation.[7]

The interdenominational Committee on Cooperation in Latin America (1913) established its office in New York.[8] Its goal was to generate cooperation among denominations and build solidarity on the American continent. This solidarity was understood as "the cordial fraternity of all the republics, of beneficial and educational forces that were devoted to save souls and alleviate the ailments of the body."[9] The contextual frame of reference was provided by Pan-Americanism, an American doctrine of cooperation embraced by the leaders of the Committee. This new Pan-Americanism, led by the United States between 1881

and 1938, was promoted by US bureaucrats but was often
denounced by Latin American intellectuals, union leaders,
nationalists, and left-leaning leaders at the time as a mechanism
to improve and stabilize economic relations between Latin
America and the United States and secure the expansion of US
interests.[10] The Committee on Cooperation was the bureaucratic base of a network that involved regional committees, the
organization of major congresses, publication of *La Nueva
Democracia* (a journal of opinion on contemporary issues from
an evangelical perspective published from 1920 to 1964), and
publication of books, congress proceedings, and reports of visits
to Latin America by key religious leaders. The Committee
organized three congresses, two of which are discussed in the
body of this paper.

These congresses were intended to generate a space for the
exchange of experiences and knowledge emerging from work
in the field as well as to build consensus[11] by promoting interaction among denominations and with lay leaders. Such discourse was expected to become an integral part of the process
of generating cooperation and unity in the missionary movement. Leaders of the Committee, such as Samuel Guy Inman,
construed the quest for unity in the missionary movement as
the religious aspect of Pan-Americanism, in a rather uncritical
manner.[12] There was also a strong sense among the leaders of
the committee and the missionaries that the missionary practice, its discourses and theological tenets, had to respond to
the need to build an identity with national components and
characteristics of the places where the various denominations
had established their missions.[13] To complicate matters
further, the overall project sponsored by the Committee on
Cooperation was strongly influenced by radical social
gospellers and theories of religious education that integrated
both pragmatists' ideas and Dewey's educational theories with
the social gospel.

In this chapter I analyze the discourses narrated in the two major congresses organized by the Committee: the Panama Congress of 1916 and the Montevideo Congress of 1925. These discourses embodied a synthetic configuration of democracy and education understood in relation to spiritual redemption, both individual and social, that was a core component of the proposed reconstruction of the Latin American polity. The two congresses addressed educational issues and clearly articulated progressive educational themes, particularly John Dewey's ideas on democracy and education, most notably at the Montevideo Congress. While social Christianity dominated the Panama Congress, a more radical (left-leaning) version of the social gospel influenced the Montevideo Congress, thereby alienating conservative evangelicals. Important issues emerged in relation to the notion of redemption (linked to conversion) and to local and regional cultural and social values, as well as to the lack of opportunities for public deliberation as understood by the missionaries. As stated in the report of the Panama Congress, "ultimate redemption must be wrought out by its own people."[14] The missionaries' understanding of redemption, however, had been imported to Latin America and was conceived as an integral part of a new process of socialization and transculturation.[15] The chapter closes with a discussion of the insights from the Havana Congress of 1929 on how to deal with problems arising from the perceived need to develop a Latin American Protestant identity.

THE PANAMA CONGRESS
(10–20 FEBRUARY 1916):
PERMEATING THE COMMUNITY WITH THE
HIGHEST CHRISTIAN IDEALS

The Panama Congress, entitled "Christian Work in Latin America," included 235 delegates representing forty-four missionary societies from the United States, one from Canada, and

five from Great Britain. There were only 27 Latin Americans in
attendance. The boards of major para-ecclesiastical, interdenominational, and non-denominational organizations were
represented, including the very radical Federal Council of the
Churches of Christ in America, the Student Volunteer Movement for Foreign Missions, the Young Men's Christian Association, the World's Woman's Christian Temperance Union, and
the World's Sunday School Association, among others. The language used at the Congress was English, which created differ-
ential possibilities for voicing views and experiences. It also
limited the delegates' capacity to understand the context that
provided or ratified meanings of the recommendations and
meant that many of them lacked an informed understanding of
the role played by related ideologies, such as Pan-Americanism,
and what the missionaries called "the sympathetic and intelligent point of view" of Latin America that informed them. Furthermore, although the sessions were presided over by Professor
Eduardo Monteverde from Montevideo, Uruguay, Rev. Robert
Speer, president of the Committee, directed the debates and
Samuel Guy Inman served as secretary. The imbalance of power
was obvious. Jean Pierre Bastian argued that the Congress was
the start of a continental evangelical movement that was conscious of its goals. However, I argue that at the Congress this
spatially organized identity (a rather abstract concept) was construed by US missionaries and the Committee on Cooperation,
whose aim was the conversion of the entire continent to a
gospel of life. This aim was pursued through the attempt to
develop the regenerating principles of a personal Christianity, a
new soul, which would also generate social changes and
progress. As Bastian wrote, it was not a coincidence that the
Congress took place in Panama, which symbolized US hege-
mony over the continent.

The missionary societies needed to re-address their work in
Latin America. Between the 1880s and 1916, the year of the
Panama Congress, most Latin American countries had gone

through a period of uneven economic development with a strong influx of American capital and dramatic social transformations and political crises. There had been a rapid process of technological modernization, including the establishment of internal and external communication systems (railways, telegraph, phone system, and ships). The continent became one of the major providers of raw materials to Europe and the US. The missions were mostly an urban phenomenon, linked to economic enclaves; they often had good relations with oligarchic governments with liberal views, and disseminated a new faith and modern values that contributed to the creation of an ideology among the emergent middle classes. The schools were a major means to Christianize and move the continent to a capitalist civilization. The educationalization of social problems mentioned by Tröhler in his chapter in this book had its own characteristics in the missionary context and education was seen as an antidote for the abuses of capitalism.[16] The Panama Congress tried to deal with the atomization of the missionaries' efforts by embracing the dominant notion of cooperation. The context in which the Congress took place included growing opposition from the left to "American imperialism" and a reaction against the perceived Americanization of the Latin American peoples, while conservative forces defended a rather idiosyncratic Hispanic and Catholic identity. The Mexican revolution (1910) had had an impact on missionaries, many of whom had been moved to join forces in spite of denominational divisions, while a large number of their national converts embraced the revolution.

The 1916 Congress in Panama was framed politically by the Mexican revolution and the developments leading to the Russian revolution of 1917. There was a sense that a major social transformation was about to happen in Latin America and many intellectuals, artists, and leaders of the time aligned themselves with socialist and anarchist movements. Meanwhile, an anti-imperialist literary movement rooted in a pan-Hispanic world view gained influence with its search for aesthetic regeneration and a concern with spirit, form, sensitivity, and a questioning of American utilitarian values.[17]

The Social Gospel, with its emphasis on regeneration and progress, had a powerful presence in American congregations and had reached the missionary field. As the secretary of the Committee put it "Latin America needs a religion that will help solve the national problems as well as those of the individuals."[18]

The Congress focused on eight themes: survey and occupation, message and method, education, literature, women's work, the church in the field, the home base, and cooperation and the promotion of unity. There was a discussion of the training and efficiency of missionaries. The "Indians," a core component of the Latin American population, are treated only tangentially in the reports of the Congress as part of the discussions on women's work and on educational issues. The missionaries' understanding of education and of the role of women in the reconstructive spiritual and social process had a central place in the redemptive discourse.

The commission that produced the Report on Education at the Congress included three professors from Teachers College at Columbia University: Professor Paul Monroe, later dean of the College; Professor James E. Russell, dean at the time of the Congress; and Professor T.H.P. Sailer. The three were later involved in reconstructionist efforts after the First World War and were familiar with progressive education. Monroe, a historian of education, was part of President Woodrow Wilson's "The Inquiry," a secret group of expert advisers that gathered from January to October 1918 to discuss prospective peace negotiations and plans for the future.[19] He was the leading educational expert in this group and reported to Walter Lippmann. Monroe emphasized the importance of integrating education with social reconstruction and with the needs of everyday life and community development and his ideas on modernization had a great deal of influence on various American initiatives in education in the international arena.[20] It is not surprising that the report reflects the ideas of John Dewey (which also appeared in some denominational and inter-denominational writings). As Lawrence Cremin puts it, "Dewey's most seminal contribution was to develop a body of pedagogical theory which could encompass the terrific diversity of the progressive education movement."[21]

Education was seen as the means to produce the new citizenry and create the new culture, which would nourish an ideal biblical, democratic polity. Furthermore, education was viewed as critical in dealing with the cultural lag resulting from the obscurantism of the Catholic Church and the persistence of political and social inequality. The report on education defined it as a process involving the interplay of the will of the individual and the will of the social group, as well as the interaction of a person and the environment. "Education is the formation of habits, the acquisition of knowledge, the development of character, all these and more according to the needs and opportunities arising from adjusting a person to his environment."[22] This definition seems somewhat paradoxical, given the context of a congress preoccupied with destroying the walls of suspicion to allow foreign intellectual, commercial, and spiritual influences to reach Latin America. The operating definition of education expounded at the Congress also recreates the same dilemma that Frederick Lilge, quoted by Cremin, believed Dewey encountered: adjusting students to the social environment could involve the integration of practices whose values had been rejected (in this case by the missionaries) or could lead teachers to sacrifice closeness to life by encouraging the students to abandon such practices. As Lilge argues, Dewey solved this dilemma, and others, by looking at a program of reforms.[23] Moreover, as David Cohen suggests, Dewey sought to create a counterculture throughout the schools that would correct the human and social devastation that had resulted from industrial capitalism.[24] Missionaries, who at this point were working within the framework of social Christianity, also conceived schools as spaces from which to challenge the dominant culture, which was influenced by the Catholic Church.

The kind of counterculture that emerged from the narrative of the participants at the Panama Congress was related to the need to respond, on one side, to the risks created by the effect of the industrial revolution on women, children, and the community and, on the other, to create a curriculum that would meet the new economic needs. The counterculture being proposed, however, was foreign, which introduced dissonance when dealing with context-dependent learning and when attempting to dovetail the narratives of progress with those of a "truly Christian civilization." Religious educator George A. Coe provided a theoretical bridge. His work combined the insights of progressive educational theorists, particularly Dewey, with the social and theological tenets of liberal Protestantism,and argued that education aims at the progressive reconstruction of society.[25] Coe summarized his thinking in a Deweyan way when he wrote in 1917 that, "education is not only society's supreme act of self-preservation; it is also society's most sincere judgment upon its own defects, and its supreme effort at self-improvement."[26]

The congressional reports relied on a notion of liberal expandable democracy and the cultivation of social conditions related to the values of modernity. The aims of educational missionary work as expounded in the reports were the "up building of the Christian community, the development of Christian leaders of spiritual power," and "the permeation of the community at large with the highest Christian ideas and ideals." These aims included a continental and even an international dimension, "to make disciples of all nations – to raise up in every nation a truly Christian people, nourished by all the fellowships and institutions of a self-propagating Christian civilization, and living in mutually helpful relations with every other people."[27] However, there were major unresolved issues involved in the exportation of a way of life. A particular problem involved the pursuit of equality for all human beings presented as a narrative that did not deal with the actual barriers of race, gender, and class or with national questions, including the issue of the American national character.

In practice, American Protestant schools in Latin America introduced innovative pedagogical methods, taught skills, and encouraged problem solving as a dimension of democratic life while trying to develop what the missionaries considered were the best elements of America to generate a new culture in Latin America, or "La America Romanista" as it was called.[28] This approach is clearly delineated in a 1924 letter addressed to friends of the Methodist Church with reference to the Lima High School in Peru, a school for girls: "But in this school the Peruvian girls are coming in contact with the very finest type of American womanhood and are being influenced by a newer and finer type of good wholesome culture than they have ever known before."[29] The political rationale behind the north-south macro power-play was being translated into the building of a transformed inner self by embracing the American values advocated by the missionaries.

Women were seen as the first educators to initiate the new generations into an understanding of the world. Thirty-two Women's Boards of Missions, either independent or auxiliary, were represented at the Panama Congress. Most of the missions had headquarters in the United States. At the time there were 418 unmarried women and widows, not including physicians, working with the boards in Latin America. The Commission on Women's Work at the Congress was made up predominantly of women from the US: 17 of whom lived in the United States, 6

in Latin America. There were also 2 Latin American women
and 2 representatives from Great Britain.

A concern with moral reform and an emphasis on chastity for
both women and men permeates the reports. The Report on
Women's Work paid particular attention to the role of the
Young Women's Christian Association, "whose scope embraces
'the young womanhood of the world'," in building new moral
foundations. At the YWCA "a new basis of congenial companionship between the sexes is created – that they may work and
play together as human beings, with equal standards of purity
for men and women, which will result in a fuller and more
perfect life for both."[30] The YWCA, as a Christian agency for
social work, provided a home for girls who had come from
some distance away and might be unprotected or without
lodging, as well as a setting in which to develop moral character. These young women were identified as being at high risk
given the "modern industrial conditions" that "throw these
girls constantly with men."[31] This moral preoccupation was
based on the notion that the home was safe while the world was
bad. Women's daily work in public places put them at risk, "the
new social liberty that has come to them, brings them into
contact with all sorts and conditions of people, and often
hideous wrongs are perpetrated on them, because they are not
safeguarded from without, as well as forewarned and forearmed
from within."[32] The culture of redemption went along with the
need to develop social plans and institutions to deal with health,
employment, and education.[33]

The report on women describes the existential conditions of
the "women of humble class," who are described as the "great
mass of humanity who bear the heaviest burdens of the race,"
with painful images of exploitation and misery. Sin and the
dominant state of morals were seen as the core of the problem,
setting the basis for regeneration and redemption. "These
women," the report reads, "bear not only the physical loads of
life, but the cruelest burden of all – that of sin; the burden of

illegitimacy brought about by the lack of any high standard of male chastity, falls most heavily on them."[34] The report quotes sources indicating that sixty out of every hundred women in the whole continent had lost self-respect and hope.[35] Miss Smith, a missionary working in Chile, pleaded for "these poor fallen girls": "Immoral? Perhaps, as we count immorality. But who of us dares to say that, given their heritage, their ignorance, their temptations, we should not have sunk so low?"[36] The plea was followed by an obvious question, asserting the role of missionary women: "Who will deny that there is work to be done for the women of Latin America?"[37] (Ironically, there were only two Latin American women at the Panama Congress.)

The "Indian women" were considered by the missionaries to form a class by themselves. Missionary work among Aboriginal peoples was often only sporadic. In the view of the missionaries, "the call of these millions of fellow Americans, many of them in pagan darkness, is one of the most compelling of our days."[38] Women were construed as those fashioning the national ideals but, with few exceptions, "Indian women were still in heathen darkness and in primitive savagery."[39] The missionaries clearly believed there was a great need to carry the Gospel to these women "who are born in paganism and who die without any knowledge of the Christ who died for them."[40]

At the time of the Panama Congress, protection of the weak, a tenet of evangelical feminism, justified the need for expertise in health education, social work, and education provided by women missionaries. This expertise secured their role in the Church and in the missionary world, where they fought for recognition of their services. Women missionaries carried out their mission not only in the name of religious truth but in the name of progress and of their ideals of womanhood, expert knowledge, and education. Their emphasis was on the ignorance of Latin American mothers. In fact, the notion of democracy as a way of life, an ideal (close to Dewey's notion of an ethical ideal) based on character and intellectual resources, as intersected in the proceedings of the Congress, conflicts with the belief in the need for the imposition of "superior" values and commitment to expertise. This overall approach was compounded by overtones of racial prejudice when dealing with Aboriginal peoples.

The educational discourse at the conference was informed by a belief in the relevance of the family, the community, and the church, which, with the state, played a major role in impressing themselves on the growing members of the community.[41] The community had a central place in the missionaries' understanding of democracy and education. The aims of education were seen in relation to modernist ideas of a balance between liberty and discipline in education. Civil order and social stability were understood as founded in custom and law. The explanation of aims concludes that "mental and spiritual fellowship among men [sic], mental and spiritual initiative and independence in the individual constitute its goal."[42] The educational method, as described in the report, should meet real situations, rely on problem solving, and develop the powers of observation, initiative, and self-reliance, and "every success should be an achievement making for intelligent self-direction."[43] These understandings are in line with the general principles of pedagogical progressive education [44] and, more specifically, with Dewey's theory of education and his notion of democracy. However, these statements are accompanied by a strong emphasis on social efficiency derived from a utilitarian vision of education in terms of governance and the structure and purpose of the curriculum. The difference between their schools and other efficiently run schools resided, in the missionaries' view, in their preoccupation with dealing with the "training of the entire man [sic], and hence must rationally include as an integral part of it moral and religious training."[45]

THE MONTEVIDEO CONGRESS
(29 MARCH TO 8 APRIL 1925):
RECONSTRUCTING THE SOCIAL ORDER AND
A RECONFIGURED MISSION

The Montevideo Congress was entitled "Christian Work in South America." One hundred and sixty-five delegates attended, forty-five of whom were Latin Americans. Only American missionaries were charged with overseeing the preparation of reports, with the exception of John A. Mackay, a Presbyterian from the Free Church of Scotland who had a close relationship with other missionaries in Peru and a political presence in that country. One of the writers was Francis J. McConnell, a distinguished Methodist as well as a high-profile social gospel leader. The Evangelical Union of South America (based in England) was represented by missionaries working in the field (Peru). As was the case during the Panama Congress, there were representatives in various capacities from para-ecclesiastical, inter-denominational, and non-denominational organizations as well as from the Comité Protestant Français and the Federation of Evangelical Churches of Spain. Although Spanish and Portuguese were the official languages, in practice the sessions were mostly in English and the reports were written in English. Also, the Latin American representatives were numerically a minority.

The context for the discussion was now fully informed by the left wing of the Social Gospel, which was embraced at the Congress. The final report, *The Church and Community*, reads: "the individualist must remember that before we can touch the inner spirit of multitudes of men [sic], we must change those outer conditions to which the social thinker is always calling attention. Since when did the relief of physical hunger cease to be in itself a worthy motive for service?"[46] These ideas and concepts are interwoven with notions of efficiency, cooperation, and progress, as well as with progressive notions of education and democracy, particularly Dewey's ideas, mostly through George A. Coe, his "translator" into the world of the social gospel. Coe's influence was not new, but was more evident in Montevideo. Donald Meyer refers to Coe as "the ablest exponent of the progressive ideas ... a student of John Dewey."[47] As Meyer noted, Coe had published his most influential book, *A Social Theory of Religious Education*, in 1917, at the same time that Walter Rauschenbusch published *A Theology for the Social Gospel*, which represented a serious effort to socialize the old doctrine by revisiting the notion of sin.[48] Rauschenbusch was actually cited in the report The *Church and Community* with reference to the understanding of social service, as was Coe.[49] Dewey's influence is not surprising since the reformers were, in Meyer's words, indebted to an age of reform and owed ideas to peoplearound; "the social gospel could be regarded as, in a sense, reform with a Protestant gloss."[50] Interestingly, Édouard Claparède, when referring to William James, wrote that all Protestantism was impregnated with the pragmatist tendency (referring to pragmatism' philosophical tenets).[51] The religious reformers' ideas were part of a synthetic configuration in which secular proposals were often translated in religious terms, and vice-versa.

By the 1920s, missionary understandings of society were in competition with other utopian visions of society as well as with popular nationalist discourses in Latin America, all of which carried pedagogical messages. As stated in the introduction to the official report, the churches were moving forward "in brave fidelity to the gospel to take their proper place in the great social movements which are pervading the whole body of South American life today."[52] In line with this approach, the Congress emphasized analysis of the organized workers' movement, the feminist movement in Latin America, and social movements such as the students' movement, university reform, and the cre-

ation of the popular universities, among others. Pan-Americanism, although mentioned, was viewed critically at the Congress.
Bishop McConnell made clear that missionary work was devoid
of political and economic purpose.[53]

Cultural nationalism of the new sort, a movement toward
homogenization of the cultural space, was exemplified by,
among others, the Mexican philosopher José Vasconcelos, who,
as minister of education for three years (1921–24) under President Obregón, had left the legacy of a cultural nationalist
program.[54] Vasconcelos, who had ambivalent relations with the
missionaries and became a member of the editorial board of *La
Nueva Democracia*, saw Latin America as a continent open to
all races and advocated a new project of life that would be
based not only on utility but also on an aesthetic sense of life.
In the 1920s there was an increasing identification of the nation
with the people (*el pueblo*).[55] The post-war period brought
social agitation among the working classes in Peru, Chile, and
Brazil. The university reform movement spread from Argentina
to most Latin American countries and generated a popular pedagogical discourse and demands that had a Latin American
dimension. It represented a major challenge to the oligarchical
liberal state, which was in the midst of a crisis.

The Protestant missions had penetrated the continent with
implicit support from oligarchic liberal governments concerned
with order and progress. In the twenties, popular nationalist
political movements and parties, such as Irigoyenismo in
Argentina, Aprismo in Peru, and internal elements of the
Partido Nacional Revolucionary in Mexico, emerged, as did
national forms of socialism, such as the development of socialism under José Carlos Mariátegui in Peru, the Communist
Party in Mexico, and more orthodox socialist approaches. The
1925 Montevideo Congress took place against that socio-political background. In fact, this Congress, like the Panama Congress, had to deal with the influence of nationalist views that
challenged American influence and the American notion of

Pan-Americanism. Interestingly most radical social gospellers were critical of American policies and influences. A number of missionaries participating in the Congress had already been involved with national leaders and had found ways to support or even influence them. A case in point is the relationship between the mission of the Methodist Episcopal Church in Peru, John Mackay, a missionary from the Free Church of Scotland and principal of the Anglo-Peruvian School, and Victor Raúl Haya de la Torre, a student leader at the time (1923) and later the founder of the American Popular Revolutionary Alliance (APRA). The influence of evangelical Protestantism on Haya may have been more than negligible.[56] The unresolved tensions among the representatives and their standpoints are somewhat apparent in the discussions in the reports and in the search for balance between individual regeneration and group regeneration.

The notion of progress was in the air and helped justify the spiritual conquest of the continent (the "spiritual conquistador" was the term used in the "Report on Religious Education"). The message of redemption and democracy and the perception of a continent at risk took on new meaning and there was an emphasis on socio-economic changes and critical glimpses of US foreign investments. This was evident in the closing remarks of Bishop Francis J. McConnell, who used a pronounced reformist language but was still aware of the difficulties that had been revealed at the Congress. One of the paragraphs reads:

> So true it is that we have assumed the soundness of the social policies announced here that we would do well to remind ourselves that the real conflict in the Christianization of the social order is to be won or lost over concrete issues. The victory over the forces which would exploit the labour, or the resource, of any class for the benefit of any other, or over the forces which would unfairly gain control of the riches of one country for the upbuilding of another,

or over the forces which for any reason would plunge nations into war, cannot be won by passing resolutions at religious congresses. Victory in any of these directions cannot be reached except as some heroic and prophetic souls are prepared to walk the way of the Cross. Still, the principles announced here concerning the social spread of the gospel of Jesus have in them terrific dynamic power. It is of immense significance that there is practical unanimity concerning them. We have come a long way from the day when such problems were looked upon as outside the realm of religious responsibility.[57]

The accent at the Congress on the social gospel generated negative reactions from independent congregations that had taken a fundamentalist turn in relation to Darwinian evolutionism.[58]

During the deliberations, the emphasis on character formation remained strong, as did the goal of generating an alternative culture, a new set of values more in tune with modern values, and a Christian understanding of democracy that involved, to an important extent, a new understanding of religion. Coe, whose work regularly reached the missionary field and whose influence on the congress was explicit, used the expression "democracy of God" rather than "kingdom of God" because the idea of democracy was, in his view, essential to understanding Jesus' teaching.[59] In *A Social Theory of Religious Education*, a book dedicated to the most radical of the social gospellers, Harry Ward, Coe talks as well of an industrial democracy, an organization of producers governed by producers.[60] He asks "Must not Christians think of God as being within human society in the democratic manner of working, helping?" He saw the ideal of a "democracy of God" as the determinant of ultimate ends in religious education; the aim of Christian education should be "Growth of the young toward and into mature and efficient devotion to the democracy of God, and happy self-realization therein."[61] Furthermore, in

Coe's view a socialized religious education could contribute to the development of a democratic state. When religious education is under the conception of the "democracy of God," he argues, "we have a socially unifying aim to which everything that is truly democratizing and humanizing in state education contributes."[62] The point here is that he does not identify religion with dogmatism and ecclesiasticism, because they are sectarian and would not make religious education suitable for public schooling. The movement toward a fully socialized religious education in public schools implied that in addition to reading, arithmetic, etc., they should teach not religion but democracy ("the democracy of God"), to make pupils democratic.[63] This was in tune with the ecumenical component of the entire social gospel movement and with the ideas of educational reformers such as William H. Kilpatrick (who, incidentally, worked with Sunday School agencies), George Counts, and, of course, John Dewey. It was not without reason that Coe had dedicated his book to Harry Ward, the most radical of the prophets, who envisioned a better world system, a "cooperative commonwealth."[64] I agree with David Setran that Coe believed that progressive educators like Dewey and Kilpatrick had discovered the essential religious nature of education and "the educational genius of true (i.e. liberal) Christianity."[65] An example of this was the focus on the child and social justice, which Coe thought had roots in Jesus' teaching. The same argument was used by Catholics inclined to use Dewey's and Kilpatrick's pedagogical theories.[66]

Character education was a major issue both in Canada and in United States after World War I and there were great debates between conservative and liberal progressives.[67] The conservatives were concerned with social changes and what they saw as the movement of the young toward social anarchy, and were eager to develop morality codes and lists of the traits of a good citizen. This approach, quite dominant at the time, was embraced by conservative churches as well. However, the missionaries and social gospel leaders at the Montevideo Congress followed Coe's lead on character education, which he conceived as part of religious education. Coe, a passionate critic of the conservative approach, opposed the notion of codified virtues and instead appealed to scientific and democratic methods to deal with moral and social issues. His books, in particular *Education in Religion and Morals,* published in 1904, were used in theological seminars in Latin America, in religious education programs, and in theological courses along with the work of W. Kirpkatrick.[68]

The Congress report on Religious Education pays particular attention to the "effective process of character education," and states that the old standbys of precept and example were inadequate. It makes two points: first, "that any character-developing process that can be consciously applied must be educational in its method; second, we learn in and through experience." Dewey's and Coe's ideas are clearly expounded in the Report:

> Experimental education confirms practical observation by insisting that character is developed and habits are formed in and through experience. It is what one does that he learns, not what he is taught; what he does with satisfaction he tends to continue, what he does with dissatisfaction he tends to avoid ... In such a process the teacher or the parent may be a comrade and guide. If the child has confidence in him, then he will be a part of the experience."[69]

Dependence on instruction separated from everyday life would not lead to "right living." The Bible is understood as a book of experience.[70] In Coe's vision of religious education, the goal was to generate a new way of being that would be a condition for the creation of the democracy of God. The main issue as revealed in the schools was how to enact these ideals in practice and develop countercultural modern values. The latter were often well received by emerging middle classes, although within the context of various understanding of democracy.[71]

Contrasting practical examples are illustrative: instead of opening exercises conducted by the superintendent of the Sunday school, a Sunday school based on activity would have the entire meeting and service conducted by the young people themselves; instead of learning how to teach by studying a book and writing correct answers, the young people would learn how to teach through practice teaching combined with observation, study, and guidance; instead of instruction that tells student what the Bible means and then questioning them to see if they "know their lesson," the young people would discuss purposes, debate the material, form judgments, and plan acts of service; instead of memorization, young people would be involved in discussion of problems rooted in their actual life and would look for Christian solutions with their leaders' cooperation; instead of a lesson selected by a committee and prepared by writers, the class would select a project that would require individual initiative and constructive activity on the part of each member.[72]

The central issue in the "Report on Religious Education" was how to relate all activities to the everyday experience of boys and girls and young people. Coe is cited there to emphasize that "within the pupil's mind the religiously educative process is religious living itself rather than something external to religion and merely preparatory to it."[73] The Report stated that "God will become real to children as He becomes a part of their experience."[74]

The educational process was conceived as being "pupil-centred rather than material-centred." There was no body of knowledge that the pupil ought to have; the planning was centred on the pupils themselves, what they were like, and what their interests, problems, and needs were. The report proposed a movement away from uniform lessons toward lessons adapted to groups of pupils with common interests, needs, and at common stages of development. It rejected the notion of presenting the Bible in historical sequence and advocated starting from the experience of the pupil looking to the Bible and other materials to enrich and direct experience. It left aside hymns and prayers that expressed adult religious experiences and developed hymns and prayers that expressed the pupils' experience. It rejected memorization of passages that were not understood, and instead emphasized understanding and application to present experiences.[75]

The report evokes what we would call nowadays a constructivist approach. The curriculum activities and materials had to meet the pupils' moral and religious needs, they had to be based on what the pupils already knew and did, pupils had to be encouraged to be aware of their environment and experience, and the methods had to be suited to their experience and capacity. The other important principle stated in the Report is that the process of character-training of the pupil should be "unified."[76]

Dewey's ideas can be seen clearly in the foregoing, although they were largely introduced through Coe's work. For example, Dewey's ideas are echoed in the notions of experience, experiential growth, and continuity, the experimental method, the understanding of the democratic (educated) person's dispositions and traits of mind, and the notion of interacting with the environment guided by experience to secure the greatest good for all. (In Latin America that environment would be a countercultural one.) Science and democracy were the tools needed to reconstruct a moral order aimed at building an active citizenry, working toward the decline of drudgery, poverty, and disease, and encouraging the rise of genius in the arts and sciences. "Freedom and order, the corner stones of democracy, are not maintained by police forces but by the ability of a citizen to govern himself."[77] This is what we would now call "regulation of the subject."

This understanding of the nature of education and the moral and social order was in line with statements made by leaders of

the Federal Council of Churches. Religion is individual in terms
of personal devotion, but "it is social in that its purpose has to
do with the redemption of the world – this present world – by
introducing a more spiritual social order."[78] The individual had
to be socialized. Meyer argued that the systematic elaboration
of these ideas was provided by the leaders in religious education
and, in particular, by Coe. Coe had integrated new psychological theories and new educational theories, specifically John
Dewey's, with the social gospel, as is evident in his books,
including *Education in Religion and Morals* published in 1904
and extensively used in the missionary field. Meyer makes the
point that the theories being advocated were those of American
pragmatism. The idea of moral biases or unchanging inner
drives was replaced by a concept of needs and energies "functioning as a complex, subject to an evolutionary development";
ideas and truth as understood by the individual were functional
and the product of interpersonal life. The personality of the self
was constituted by habits and convictions that developed
through the process of acceptance and rejection of ideas.[79] The
notion of human nature as pure potentiality was interpreted by
pragmatists like Dewey and by Coe as being morally positive.[80]
This articulation of the pragmatists' ideas and of social gospel
positions as expressed in religious education generated innovative practices in missionary schools, which became sites of political formation. The schools also provided skills needed in the
emergent if uneven capitalist economy in Latin America.[81]

It is not surprising that the "Report on Religious Education"
shows a seamless articulation of humanity, God, and the world,
an articulation that Dewey had questioned in 1908 in "Religion
and Our Schools" when critiquing religious educators.[82]
However, Dewey did not close the doors on religion. He concluded the article by saying:

So far as education is concerned, those who believe in religion as a natural expression of human experience must

devote themselves to the development of the ideas of life which lie implicit in our still new science and our still newer democracy. They must interest themselves in the transformation of those institutions which still bear the dogmatic and the feudal stamp (and which do not?) till they are in accord with these ideas. In performing this service, it is their business to do what they can to prevent all public educational agencies from being employed in ways which inevitably impede the recognition of the spiritual import of science and of democracy, and hence of that type of religion which will be the fine flower of the modern spirit's achievement.[83]

The interdenominational movement was far from promoting the type of "religion" mentioned by Dewey, but its leaders did not seem concerned with the tension it created with their own position. Dewey's statement could have been interpreted as acknowledging the possibility of a spiritualization of freedom through science and democracy. In the same article, however, Dewey was critical of the view that religion was a universal function of life.

In the Congress's report on religious education, the emphasis on scientific problem solving went along with the notion that the very essence of the universe is divine purpose and that this essence is something we experience. Practice in experiencing fellowship with the divine whole would secure the moral power necessary to discover and to attain new and needed ideals. In the deliberations of the congresses and in Coe's work the intersection of the social gospel and pragmatist theories and Dewey's educational theories is construed as the means to social reconstruction, redemption, and the realization of a new democratic polity. The main unresolved tension here is between redemption and democratic means, the breakdown between means and ends that Johnston discusses in his chapter in this book. One can think of redemption by and large as implying some kind of conversion, including a religious one; this process did not necessarily entail democratic means. Means and ends are conflated. The treatment of Aboriginal issues, discussed later, can be seen as an example of this. A further complication was an uncritical reliance on Pan-Americanism on the part of the leaders of the Interdenominational Committee, which brought a particular pro-American political dimension to the notion of redemption, one not necessarily accepted by the most radical social gospellers present at the Montevideo Congress.

Coe, as were the major exponents of the social gospel, was also preoccupied with the "public mind" and how to change the public mindset in the tactical pursuit of social change.[84] In the US the social gospel's public were members of suburban, small city, small town, and even rural communities in the East and especially in the Midwest. The public mind was grounded, Meyer wrote, in the culture-community.[85] In Latin America the presence of Protestantism had been by and large an urban phenomenon and Protestant schools had helped create a new middle class.

The challenge at the Montevideo Congress was to reach the Aboriginal peoples and those in rural areas, and to deal with a growing national consciousness even among converts. Changing the public mindset as understood by the missionaries in Latin America demanded the development of new values and habits that were somewhat disconnected from lived experiences and, ultimately, conversion to a new religion. The concept of the public, among even the most progressive missionaries, was far from Dewey's notion of individuals who could use scientific inquiry as a means to democratic living. Furthermore, the missionaries' ethnocentric universalizing approach did not leave much room to articulate world views constructed in particular socio-cultural settings other than those of the eager emerging middle classes. Thus Bishop McConnell, aware of the lack of agencies "that quicken the public conscience on great moral issues," emphasized the responsibility of the evangelical pulpit.[86]

The Congress fully embraced the equal rights feminist agenda and went beyond the protection of sisters at risk. The report reads: "Since Christ Himself made no unequal distinctions between men and women, the Evangelical forces should educate public opinion to stand squarely for equal rights and duties of men and women before the law, and for an equal standard of morality in its highest interpretation."[87] It found a parallel between the notion of the role of women in building a renewed society and Coe's appeal "to abandon the doctrine and the practice of the inequality of the sexes" in a democratic family.[88] The Congress paid great attention to the feminist movement in Latin America and there are references to Pan-American child congresses.[89] The report on unoccupied fields refers to the phenomenal rise of the feminist movement and its passion for social justice, which promised ethical enrichment and increased social efficiency for South American culture. Most denominations either had schools for girls or coeducation in their schools. Pedagogical practices linking knowledge to experience, the schools to the community, and the mediation of scientific methods to the solution of problems were analyzed by various participants. However, the role of women in the overall vision of the missionaries remained unclear or contradictory. The question of equal rights and duties, strongly addressed in the resolutions, coexisted with the cult of domesticity and with the notion of the woman as guardian of the social order. The aims of one of the most progressive schools, Lima High School in Peru, were explained as follows:

> Thus, we have tried to guide them to choose a noble and serving vocation, to inculcate in them the highest ideals of the dignity of the home, to cultivate good habits of self-discipline and intellectual independence, to awaken in them

respect towards all races, to recognize the right of each individual to enjoy social, economic and religious freedom and finally to teach them to accept their social responsibility without prejudices or discriminations, with love to humanity in its entirety.[90]

The most unresolved of the issues addressed by the missionaries was the evangelization of the Aboriginal peoples, who are referred to as the Indians of South America, the neglected other. This issue brings to the front race relations and the missionaries' understandings of the issue at home. The Aboriginal people were often referred to as primitive and simple minded. In the missionaries' view "All these children of God must be won to conscious fellowship in the great family of which God is the Father, and of whom all the families of earth are named."[91] One of the missionaries stated that "there is no question that the Indian makes a fine citizen and a good Christian when he has a chance."[92] Race blindness and the lack of openness toward integrating other cultural values were grounded on the universality of the missionaries' progressive vision. Coe, who developed the concept of "democracy of God" and thought of religious education as going beyond the denominations and having a socially unifying aim to democratize and humanize education at the public level, seldom mentioned the issue of race. His solution was based on interaction of the various racial groups, who would realize their unity in relation to a common devotion to freedom.[93]

It was believed that the missions would act as a social agency in the civilizing project aimed at awakening Aboriginal peoples to new ways of living and to new ideals and to integrating them in the life of the nations through education and services.[94] It was an ethical ideal permeated by a notion of democracy. There was, however, a clear imposition of values even through newly construed lived experience; this is where Dewey's thinking clearly differed from the missionaries, whose ultimate goal was conversion. The strategies explored by the missionaries to reach their objectives included trying to influence the upper classes, negotiating meanings with social and political leaders, such as Haya de la Torre in Peru and José Vasconcelos or the Presbyterian Moisés Saenz in Mexico, and building a new middle class while reaching out to the Aboriginal peoples and the poor in rural areas. In the end, in most cases they exercised their influence through a wide range of schools with differing mandates, from the Presbyterian Instituto Inglés in Santiago, Chile, through the Presbyterian popular schools in Valparaiso (south of Chile), which were characterized by low fees, and the schools for Aboriginals in Paraguay, founded by the American Missionary Society of the Anglican Church, to the various Methodist schools in Peru, which were mainly vocationally oriented. The emphasis often placed by Protestant schools on the teaching of English and commercial subjects was in line with the needs of foreign capital and with the notion that living a worthwhile life also included training in some particular field.[95]

The Montevideo Congress was followed by the Havana Congress in 1929, which was limited to Central America and led by Latin Americans. Although the basic tenets of Social Gospel and progressive education were acknowledged, a politically conservative tone seemed to permeate the summary report (the record of the Congress). The spirit of the Congress was affected by the realization that Protestant churches had been unable, by and large, "to build ties with our people," that is, the Latin American people.[96] A modicum of success in forming collaborations with nationals at particular political junctures, a sizeable number of converts, and influence on the community through school work and other services seemed to be far from the projected goals. The missionaries' work had remained within an unrooted theological configuration with only fragile ties to Latin American ideas and reality. This situation led Protestant liberation theologian José Miguez Bonino to complain bitterly in 1970 about the theological sterility still dominant in Latin America after five hundred years of Christian presence, including one hundred years of Protestantism.[97]

CLOSING THOUGHTS

The Committee on Cooperation in Latin America tried to develop a common discourse among missionaries as part of an eclectic modernist configuration. It synthesized political agendas, such as the uncritical adoption of Pan-Americanism, with moderate social gospel theological tenets and an updated version of political liberalism in the realm of progressive theory. The Congresses generated discourses that created instability in the overall configuration of ideas that served as a reference horizon in an attempt to articulate a spiritualized notion of democracy and education. Protestant schools, religious education through various avenues, and lectures were seen as the main ways of reaching the public and generating a new way of life, a new polity, a Protestant liberal democracy, a counterculture. The Panama Congress and the Montevideo Congress had evident ideological differences deriving from contesting theological interpretations, as well as differing understandings emerging from the interaction with the political culture in Latin America and the presence and voice of a new set of actors, the converts. The latter did not have full access, because of language, to the deliberations of the Congresses, which were mostly in English, and were numerically in a minority position even at the Montevideo Congress. However, they had their own experiences, often emotional ones that involved conflicting feelings about political and cultural domination and the religious and democratic ideals that provided the basis of their understandings. In some places, such as the case of Mexico, the converts served as political bridges between the missionaries and and the post-revolutionary Mexican leadership. The Panama

Congress relied on social Christianity or a moderate version of the social gospel as well as progressive education (in particular Dewey's ideas) and the goal of building a new polity based on a notion of personal redemption with social connotations. The Montevideo Congress introduced a strong reconstructionist (melliorist) progressive discourse rooted in a social gospel with radical overtones and strong social redemptive components. The actors at the Montevideo Congress appropriated Dewey's concepts through the work of George Coe, who integrated Dewey's ideas and psychology with the social gospel. Coe's approach to religious education was permeated by his notion of democracy as the democracy of God. However, the report on religious education, although rich in Coe's ideas, had an abstract tone. In the reports of the Congress, there was poor theological and political articulation of local and regional political configurations and emerging "indigenous" notions of democracy. Although the reports of both congresses contain lengthy analyses of the situation in Latin America and of various social and political movements, they have a detached character, a tone of otherness, that becomes particularly evident in the treatment of the Aboriginal peoples. In the end, the missionaries tried to bring what they considered was the best of the United States to the Americas, to build a new culture in tune with their vision for their own country and their perceived role as world leaders. The merging of progressive conceptions of democracy and education with a missionary vision for Latin America configured a unique space that took shape in missionary schools as well as in Sunday schools. The discourse populating that configuration and even pedagogical practices was framed by missionaries' and converts' experience in the field and, often, by the need to acknowledge the presence in Latin America of political projects and social movements whose goals and boundaries changed quickly and became nationalistic and politically radical.

The discourse at the congresses reveals a prophetic project to redeem a continent believed to be at risk of not developing its humanity, of not knowing Christ and his message of salvation, of not developing a liberal biblical democracy, of living in darkness and sin. It was a reconstructive project of redeeming the social and individual soul, rooted in a Protestant interpretation of a liberal, progressive, expandable democracy and a concern with the individual as a social being. The Montevideo Congress, in particular, had a strong reconstructionist approach.

The appropriation of Dewey's notion of democracy as a form of life became spiritualized to the point that democracy became synonymous with Protestant liberal Christianity.[98] The ideal Christian student was one able to reconcile religious experience with the scientific method and engagement with the world. The conception of education described in the reports produced by the congresses and its emphasis on social interaction, cooperation, and inquiry methods were part of the reformist Protestant Christian utopian vision, which had a militant, conquering character in spite of its historical fragility. The intersection of the social gospel and progressive education, in particular Dewey's ideas and his pragmatist philosophy, provided the means to develop that vision, which emerged timidly at the Panama Congress but reached full force at the Montevideo Congress.

The main problem with the comprehensive configuration and its goals was captured in a statement made at the Havana Congress in 1929, "We are strange to our race." In other words, Protestantism and its project were by and large perceived by Latin Americans in the early twentieth century as a foreign import, despite efforts to secure a social presence in the continent. At that point in history, modern universalism was trumped by the complex and diverse historical reality of Latin America, including the powerful presence of Catholicism and the limits on the exportation of democracy. The latter idea was

entangled with the United States' vision of itself as a leading
political and economic power and its interventionist history in
the Americas.

NOTES

1   Doug Rossinow, "The Radicalization of the Social Gospel: Harry F.
    Ward and the Search for a New Social Order, 1898–1936," *Religion
    and American Culture: A Journal of Interpretation* 15, no.1 (2005):
    63–106. Reference on 63.

2   The methodological approach introduced by Jürgen Schriewer is a
    good point of reference here. See Jürgen Schriewer, "Multiple Inter-
    nationalities: The Emergence of a World-Level Ideology and the Per-
    sistence of Idiosyncratic World Views." In Christophe Charle, Jürgen
    Schriewer, and Peter Wagner, eds, Transnational Intellectual Net-
    works: Forms of Academic Knowledge and the Search for Cultural
    Identities ,473–534. (Frankfurt/New York: Campus Verlag, 2004).

3   Panama Congress 1916. Christian Work in Latin America (New
    York, The Missionary Education Movement, 1917), vol. 1, 4.

4   Ibid., 8.

5   Ibid., 9–10.

6   For an analysis of the ideology of racial Anglo-Saxonism, see Regi-
    nald Horsman, *Race and Manifest Destiny: The Origins of American
    Racial Anglo-Saxonism* (Cambridge: Harvard University Press,
    1981).

7   See Rossinow, "The Radicalization of the Social Gospel," 64.

8   In 1916, the Panama Congress made the Committee on Cooperation
    in Latin America a permanent body. See also Panama Congress 1916,
    vol. 1 of *Christian Work in Latin America,* (New York: The Mission-
    ary Education Movement, 1917), 9; Rosa Bruno-Jofré, *Methodist
    Education in Peru: Social Gospel, Politics, and American Ideological
    and Economic Penetration, 1888–1930* (Waterloo, Canada: Wilfrid
    Laurier University Press, 1988), 46–7.

9 J.O.G, "Qué es el Comité de Cooperación en la América Latina?" *El Mensajero* 6, 62 (Lima, June 1920), 16. See also Panama Congress, vol. 1, 3, and 9.

10 The first of the modern Pan-American Conferences took place in Washington, DC (1889–90). At that conference the Commercial Bureau of the American Republics, which became the Pan-American Union, was created. There were a number of organizations dealing with specific areas such as the Pan-American Health Organization, the International American Institute for the Protection of Children, the Inter-American Commission of Women, the Inter-American Indigenist Institute, etc.

11 For a theoretical discussion see Bernard Lahire, ed., *Le travail sociologique de Pierre Bourdieu. Dettes et critiques* (Paris, 2001).

12 The understanding of Protestantism as the religious aspect of Pan-Americanism was developed by Samuel G. Inman, executive secretary of the Committee. See also Braga Monteverde, *Pan-Americanismo, Aspecto Religiosos* (New York: Sociedad para la Educacion Misionera, 1917).

13 Jean Pierre Bastian, *Breve Historia del Protestantismo en America Latina* (Mexico: Casa Unida de Publicaciones, 1986), 111–12.

14 Panama Congress 1916, vol. 11 of *Christian Work in Latin America* (New York: The Missionary Education Movement, 1917), 184.

15 The focus was on American culture and values; the United States was also the political point of reference. For an understanding of the transatlantic community of discourse in philosophy and politics see James T. Kloppenberg, *Uncertain Victory: Social Democracy and Progressivism in European and American Thought, 1870–1920* (New York and Oxford: Oxford University Press, 1986) and Daniel T. Rodgers, *Atlantic Crossings: Social Politics in a Progressive Age* (Cambridge, MA, and London, UK: Harvard University Press, 1998).

16 Daniel Tröhler, "Marxism or Protestant Democracy? The Pragmatist Response to the Perils of Metropolis and Modern Industry in the Late 19th Century," Paper presented at ISCHE 2007: Children and Youth at Risk, University of Hamburg, 25–28 July 2007.

17 See Alberto Prieto-Calixto, "Rubén Darío and Literary Anti-Ameri-
    canism/Anti-Imperialism," in *Beyond the Ideal, Pan Americanism in
    Inter-American Affairs*, ed. David Sheinin (Westport, CT, London:
    Praeger, 2000), 57–67.

18 Samuel Guy Inman, *Christian Cooperation in Latin America: Report
    of a Visit to Mexico, Cuba and South America, March-October, 1917*
    (New York, NY: Committee on Cooperation in Latin America, 1917),
    19.

19 David Ment, "Education, Nation-Building and Modernization after
    World War I: American Ideas for the Peace Conference," *Paedagogica
    Historica* 41, nos. 1 & 2 (2005): 159–77.

20 Ibid.

21 Lawrence Cremin, "John Dewey and the Progressive Education
    Movement, 1915–1952," in *Dewey on Education,* ed. Reginald D.
    Archambault (New York, NY: Random House, 1966), 13.

22 Panama Congress, *Christian Work,* 1: 501.

23 Cremin, "John Dewey and the Progressive Education Movement,"
    22–3.

24 David K. Cohen, "Dewey's Problem," *Elementary School Journal* 98,
    no. 5 (1998).

25 George A. Coe (1862–1951) graduated from the University of
    Rochester with a BA in 1884 and an MA in 1888. He did a BST in
    1887 and his PHD in 1891. From 1890 to 1891 he studied at the Uni-
    versity of Berlin. He changed his professional interest from philoso-
    phy to experimental psychology early in his career and by the begin-
    ning of the twentieth century he was very much involved with
    religious education. He taught at the University of Southern Califor-
    nia (1888–90), Northwestern University, where he held the John
    Evans Professorship in Moral and Intellectual Education (1893 to
    1909), Union Theological Seminary (1909–22), and Teachers College
    of Columbia University (1911–1927). He was one of the founders of
    the Religious Education Association of America. His papers are at the
    Northwestern University Archives, Evanston, Illinois.

26 George Albert Coe, *A Social Theory of Religious Education*, 2nd ed.

(New York, NY: Charles Scribner's Sons, 1927), 18. Coe wrote that Dewey had put education and industrial democracy into a single perspective.

27 Panama Congress, *Christian Work*, 1:504.

28 Letter of Clyde W. Brewster, Methodist Episcopal Mission, addressed to "My Dear Friends," dated Huancayo-Peru, 1 March 1924.

29 Ibid.

30 Panama Congress, *Christian Work*, 2:171.

31 Ibid.

32 Ibid.

33 Ibid., 133.

34 Ibid., 134.

35 Ibid.

36 Ibid.

37 Ibid.

38 Ibid., 136.

39 Ibid., 137.

40 Ibid.

41 Ibid., 1:501.

42 Ibid., 502.

43 Ibid., 503.

44 The notion of pedagogical progressive education is taken from David Labaree, who differentiates between pedagogical and administrative progressives in education. David. F. Labaree, "Progressivism, Schools, and Schools and Education: An American Romance,"*Paedagogica Historica* 41, nos. 1, 2 (February 2005): 280.

45 Panama Congress, *Christian Work*, 505.

46 Montevideo Congress 1925, in vol. 2, *Christian Work in South America* (New York, NY/Chicago, IL: Fleming H. Revell Company, 1925), 46–7.

47 Donald Meyer, *The Protestant Search for Political Realism, 1919–1941*, 2nd ed. (Middletown, CT: Wesleyan University Press, 1988), 137.

48 Meyer writes that "Rauschenbusch pointed to the sinfulness that pre-

cedes all acts of sin, provoked in every individual by the sinful acts and conditions of others around him. The particular form taken by sin in the individual was simply a function of the form it took in his social group." Ibid., 131.

49 Montevideo Congress, *Christian Work*, 2:37.

50 Meyer, *The Protestant Search*, 2.

51 Ed. Claparède, *L'education fonctionnelle*, 6th ed. (Neuchâtel, Switzerland: Delachaux et Niestlé, 1968), 24.

52 Montevideo Congress, *Christian Work*, 1:22.

53 Montevideo Congress, *Christian Work*, 2:71.For an understanding of the complex relations of post-revolutionary Mexican leaders and the Protestants see Daniel R. Miller, "Protestantism and Radicalism in Mexico from the 1860s to the 1930s," *Fides et Historia* 40, no. 1 (Winter/Spring 2008): 22. Jean-Pierre Bastian, *Los disidentes: Sociedades protestantes y revolución en México, 1872–1911* (México D.F.: Fondo de Cultura Económica y El Colegio de México, 1989).Rosa Bruno-Jofre and Carlos Martínez Valle, Ruralizando a Dewey: El amigo Americano, colonización interna, y la Escuela de la Acción en México pos-revolucionario. *Encounters/Encuentros/Rencontres Education,* fall 2009, 43–64.

54 Carlos Martínez, personal communication, 20 June 2008. He argues that the project to incorporate the masses encountered the heterogeneity of the Aboriginal population as well as the influence of the Catholic Church and its resistance.

55 See Jean Franco, *La Cultura Moderna en América Latina* (México, Barcelona, Buenos Aires: Grijalbo, 1985), 90–5.

56 See Rosa Bruno-Jofré, *Methodist Education in Peru;* John H. Sinclair and Juan A. Mackay, "Un Escocés con Alma Latina, México" (D.F. México: CUPS, 1990).

57 Montevideo Congress, *Christian Work*,1:33.

58 Bastian, Breve Historia, 119.

59 David P. Setran, "Morality for the 'Democracy of God': George Albert Coe and the Liberal Protestant Critique of American Character Education, 1917–1940," *Religion and American Culture: A*

Journal of Interpretation 15, no. 1 (2005): 113. See George A. Coe, *A Social Theory of Religious Education,* 2nd ed. (New York: Charles Scribner's Sons, 1927), 54–5.

60 Ibid., 16.

61 Ibid., 55.

62 Ibid., 262–3.

63 Ibid.

64 Rossinow, "The Radicalization of the Social Gospel," 77.

65 Setran, "Morality for the 'Democracy of God'," 112.

66 Rosa Bruno-Jofré and Gonzalo Jover, "The Readings of John Dewey's Work: The Cases of the Institución Libre de Enseñanza and the Thesis on Dewey of Father Alberto Hurtado, S.J." Manuscript submitted for publication.

67 Setran, "Morality for the 'Democracy of God'," 108. With reference to Canada see "Report of the Proceedings of the National Conference on Character Education in Relation to Canadian Citizenship" (Winnipeg, 1919).

68 Montevideo Congress, *Christian Work,* 2:128, 131, and 132.

69 Montevideo Congress, *Christian Work,*2:88.

70 Ibid.

71 See Bruno-Jofré, *Methodist Education in Peru,* and Jether Pereira Ramalho, *Prática Educativa e Sociedade: Um Estudo de Sociologia da Educacao* (Rio de Janeiro, Brazil: Zahar Editores, 1976).

72 Montevideo Congress, *Christian Work,* 2:89–90.

73 Ibid., 90.

74 Ibid.

75 Ibid., 91.

76 Ibid.

77 Ibid., 81–2.

78 Quoted from Meyer, *The Protestant Search for Political Realism,* 136.

79 Ibid., 137–8.

80 Ibid., 138.

81 For example, for a study of Protestant schools in Brazil see Jether Pereira Ramalho, *Prática Educativa e Sociedade;* Jether Pereira

Ramalho, "The Pedagogical Characteristics of Protestant Schools and the Ideological Categories of Liberalism," in *Protestant Educational Conceptions, Religious Ideology and Schooling Practices, Monographs in Education* 22, eds. Jean Pierre Bastian and Rosa Bruno-Jofré (Winnipeg, Manitoba: University of Manitoba, 1994), 61–75; Antonio Gouvea Mendoca, *Ideology and Protestant Religious Education in Brazil*, in ibid., 76–106; Jean Pierre Bastian, *Ideals of Protestant Womanhood, Religious Ideology, and the Education of Women in Mexico, 1880–1910*, in ibid., 107–31.

82 Helen Allan Archibald, "Originating Vision and Visionaries of the REA," *Religious Education* 98, no. 4 (Fall 2003): 422.

83 "John Dewey, Religion and Our Schools," *Hibbert Journal* (July 1908); reprinted in Joseph Ratner, ed. *Intelligence in the Modern World: John Dewey's Philosophy* (New York: Random House, 1939), 715.

84 Meyer, *The Protestant Search*, 110.

85 Ibid.

86 Montevideo Congress, *Christian Work*, 2:73.

87 Montevideo Congress, *Christian Work*, 1:454–5.

88 Coe, *A Social Theory of Religious Education*, 211. First edition 1917.

89 For a comprehensive view of the Pan American child congresses see Donna J. Guy, "The Pan American Child Congresses, 1916 to 1942: Pan Americanism, Child Reform, and the Welfare State in Latin America," *Journal of Family History* 23, no. 3 (July 1998): 272–91.

90 Jane Hahne, "A Todas y Cada una de las Ex-Alumnas del Lima High School. Blue and Gold," special number, 50th anniversary, Lima (21 June 1956), 16. See Bruno-Jofré, *Methodist Education in Peru* and also "Protestant Educational Conceptions, Religious Ideology and Schooling Practices: Selected papers," *University of Manitoba, Monographs in Education* 22 (1994), eds. Bastian and Bruno-Jofré.

91 Montevideo Congress, *Christian Work*, 1:151.

92 Ibid., 215.

93 Coe, *A Social Theory of Religious Education*, 263. See also George A. Coe, *Educating for Citizenship* (New York: Charles Scribner's Sons 1934), 175.

94 Ibid., 152, 153.

95 Bruno-Jofré, *Methodist Education in Peru*, 142.

96 Gonzalo Baez Camargo, *Hacia la Renovación Religiosa en Hispanoamérica* (Mexico: CUPSA, 1930), 54.

97 José Miguez Bonino, Prologue to *Rubem Alves, Religión: Opio o Instrumento de Liberación* (Montevideo: Tierra Nueva 1970)i-ii, cited in Leopoldo Cervantes-Ortiz, "Génesis de la Nueva Teología Protestante Latinoamericana (1949–1970)," II Simposio Internacional sobre Historia del Protestantismo en América Latina, San Cristóbal de las Casas, Chiapas (October 20, 2004).

98 Archibald in "Originating" refers to how Coe spiritualized democracy, 421.

Index